Albert G. Robinson

The Porto Rico of To-Day

Pen pictures of the people and the country

Albert G. Robinson

The Porto Rico of To-Day

Pen pictures of the people and the country

ISBN/EAN: 9783337427603

Printed in Europe, USA, Canada, Australia, Japan

Cover: Foto ©Andreas Hilbeck / pixelio.de

More available books at **www.hansebooks.com**

THE PORTO RICO OF TO-DAY

*PEN PICTURES OF THE PEOPLE
AND THE COUNTRY*

BY

ALBERT GARDNER ROBINSON

NEW YORK
CHARLES SCRIBNER'S SONS
1899

PREFATORY NOTE

IN the preparation of this book, it has not been the purpose of the writer to produce a guide-book, an economic treatise, or a hand-book of military science. Yet all these, and other topics, are treated with more or less fulness in its pages. The work is based upon a series of letters furnished to *The Evening Post* of New York, during the months of August, September, and October, 1898, which have been revised and amplified for this purpose. As a correspondent for that paper, the writer accompanied one of the first detachments of the army of invasion to Porto Rico, and remained on the island until after the conclusion of the campaign by the raising of the American flag over the city of San Juan, on October 18th. The purpose of this book then is to present a picture of the people and of the country as the author saw them, and to throw light upon the commercial possibilities in our new possession that lie within the reach of American business men.

A. G. R.

CONTENTS

I

PREPARATIONS FOR THE CAMPAIGN

Marching Orders — The Composition and Command of the Porto Rico Expedition—Uncertainty Regarding its Movement—Confusion of Orders — The Embarkation from Tampa, . . *Page 1*

II

LIFE ON A TROOP-SHIP

Some Faults in Troop Transportation—Unnecessary Exposure to Danger—Soldiers Killing Time—Grumbling at the Commissary —Food of Officers and Privates—A Midnight Excitement— Encounter with the Eagle on the Blockading Line—Arrival at Ponce, ... *Page 11*

III

EARLY DAYS ON THE ISLAND

Porto Rico or Puerto Rico—The Carib Title—Boriquén—First Impressions of the Island—The Harbor of Ponce—Unloading Transports — Soldiers as Stevedores — Mutual Curiosity—La Playa—The City of Ponce—Appearance of the Common People —Pedlers—The Island Ponies—Shopping Experiences—Courtesy from a Citizen, ... *Page 26*

IV

THE CITY OF PONCE

Our Reception—Busy Days—Two Centres of Activity—Amusements—Police Department—Fire Department—The Market—Ponce Stores—A Lesson in Spanish, ... *Page 47*

V

INTO THE COFFEE DISTRICT

The Town of Yauco—The Sunday Morning Market—Fruits and Vegetables—Jacky and the Natives—Guanica—Our First Landing Place—A Horse Trade—On the Road to Adjuntas—A Mountain Town—The Good Padre—The Kitchen-maid and her Cigar, ... *Page 62*

VI

A NIGHT IN THE SADDLE

Correspondents on the Firing-line—An Excited Chief of Police—Beyond the Outposts—A Search for Willing Prisoners—A Blind Trail—A Spaniard's Hospitality—Midnight Encounters—Friends or Foes—Unwilling Rough Riders—A Striking Picture—The Capture—"Too Near" Home, ... *Page 78*

VII

TYPICAL TOWNS AND VILLAGES

"Shucks and Shacks"—Picturesque San German—"Hotel the Struggle"—A Restless Night—A Native Description of the Engagement at Hormigueros—Two Humble Heroes—A Notable Shrine—Beautiful Mayaguez—A Miniature Street-car Line—Public Buildings—The Casino, ... *Page 93*

VIII

FROM PONCE TO SAN JUAN

A Model Highway—A Bicycle Trip Worth Taking—Island Villages—The Baths of Coamo—Good Luck for our Army—A Mountain Drive—Passing the Outposts—Cayey and Guayama—Nature's Bounty—System of Road Repairs—Porto Rican Roadhouses, ... *Page 108*

IX

HIGHWAYS

An Important Factor in Island Development—Present Highway System—A Hard Journey—The Bovimotor—The Boy and the Coachman—Fun for the Boy, and Entertainment for the Audience—Porto Rican Drivers—The Need of Good Roads—Costly Transportation—A Heavy Charge on Industries, . . *Page 122*

X

RAILROADS AND TELEGRAPHS

The Railways of To-day—The Ponce and Yauco Division—The Humiliation of a Traveller—The Solitary Occupant of the Apartment of the First Class—Familiar Sights in a Foreign Land—The Requirements of the Island—Present System of Transportation—Probable Benefits of Railway Extension—The United States in the Telegraph Business—Cable Lines, ... *Page 135*

XI

INDUSTRIAL POSSIBILITIES

Our New Farm—Mining Possibilities and Timber Lands—The Outlook for Sugar—The Coffee Industry—Encouragement in Tobacco-growing—Obstacles to Export Fruit Trade—Cattle-raising—An American Bermuda—Victims of Mañana, . . . *Page 150*

XII

COMMERCE ON THE ISLAND

Ephemeral Trade—Problems for the Merchants—Arrival of the Commercial Army—Disappointed Speculators and Promoters—Local Productions—The Volume of Imports—The Export Trade—Porto Rican Business Methods—Influence of Tariff—Outlook for Americans, ... *Page 163*

XIII

OLLA PODRIDA

The Best Way to Travel on the Island—Sleeping Accommodations—Conservative Farmers—Food Staples of the Peasantry—The Temperature and Its Results—The Educational Question—Schools and School-houses of San Juan—Points of Interest—Pretty Girls—Cost of City Government—The "Color" Question—Porto Rican Homes, , ... *Page 180*

XIV

THE CAMPAIGN ON THE ISLAND

Military Skill *vs.* the "Dispensations of Providence"—The Plan of the Porto Rico Campaign—A Unique Expedition—General Schwan's Sweep to the West—Difference in American and Spanish Methods in Warfare—Discomforts of a Tropical Campaign—An Unwritten Story—Our Insignificant Casualties, . *Page 197*

XV

UNDER THE OLD RÉGIME

Exaggerated Idea of Spanish Oppression—Heavily Taxed, but Virtually Free from Debt—A Citizen's Complaints—A Nineteenth Century Inquisition—Taxes for Special Purposes—Annexation Preferred to Autonomy—The Hope of the People, . , . . . *Page 206*

XVI

ADIOS! ESPAÑA

A Brief but Impressive Ceremony—The De Profundis of Spanish Rule—Amicable Relations—Admiral Sampson's System of Ventilation for Public Buildings—The Fortifications of San Juan—The Soldiers of the Boy King—Their Repatriation—The Law of Karma, ... *Page 219*

LIST OF ILLUSTRATIONS

Facing page

Palace of the Governor-General, San Juan, now the American Official Head-Quarters	*Frontispiece*
United States Transports off Port Ponce	28
A Typical Street in Port Ponce	32
A Street Scene in Port Ponce	36
Main Road, Ponce to Port Ponce	40
A Street in Ponce	52
View of Ponce from the Hospital	56
Market-Place at Ponce	64
Cathedral and Plaza at Arecibo	80
Dominican Monastery, in San German, Built about 1511	96
Plaza and City Hall in San German	100
Cathedral and Plaza at Ponce	110
The Military Road near Ponce	116
The Military Road from Ponce to San Juan	120
Where the Natives Live	132
The Home of a Planter	154
Home of the Peons	172
Looking Westward from Fort San Cristobal—Morro in the Distance	190
Looking Eastward from Morro—San Cristobal in the Distance	190

LIST OF ILLUSTRATIONS

Facing page

Ruins of Passenger-Cars Burned by the Spaniards at Ponce . 198

Commanding Officers of the Twenty-fifth Alphonso Guard, in front of the Spanish Barracks, Arecibo 204

Seventh United States Artillery, Light Battery M, Encamped near Ponce 206

Fort San Cristobal, San Juan 222

Plaza in San Juan, with the City Hall on the Left . . . 226

St. John's Church, San Juan, showing the Effects of the Bombardment 230

MAPS

General Map of Porto Rico . . . . *At end of volume*
Telegraph Lines and Stations in Porto Rico . " " "
Porto Rico and its Coast Line . . . . " " "

THE PORTO RICO OF TO-DAY

I

PREPARATIONS FOR THE CAMPAIGN

Marching Orders — The Composition and Command of the Porto Rico Expedition — Uncertainty Regarding its Movement — Confusion of Orders — The Embarkation from Tampa.

New York, June 3, 1898.

A. G. Robinson,
 Chattanooga, Tenn.

Leave for Jacksonville immediately to join Lee's expedition to Porto Rico. Report by wire on arrival there.

The Evening Post.

FOR the six weeks preceding the receipt of this telegram I had been engaged in studying and reporting the conditions of the life of our troops at Camp Thomas. It had been arranged that I should accompany the army to Porto Rico whenever it should start. Within three hours of the receipt of this message I was on my way to Jacksonville, Fla., then the head-quarters of the Seventh Army Corps, General Fitzhugh Lee commanding. I obeyed the first four words of my instructions, but I was more than doubtful of any opportunity to obey the following seven. But at that time Washington and New York had accepted the rumor that Lee and the Seventh Corps were to invade and occupy the island of Porto Rico. The move on Porto Rico had been discussed and planned, and there was some ground for expectation of its immediate development. That the move would be made under the command of General Lee was not the logic of the situation, although many of our people and many of our leading journals fully believed that Lee was slated for that expedition.

Lee's proper and logical destination was Havana, to which point he was ordered later on, and not San Juan, where rumor at this time had assigned him. He knew Havana, had been there during the days of special stress, had left there under peculiar circumstances, and, on leaving, had told the Havanese—though his statement was rather personal than official—that he would come back to them with an army behind him. It therefore seemed wholly fitting that if Havana were to be made a point of attack during the impending war, General Lee's words on leaving that city should be made good by the government which sent him there. There were other reasons also why the Seventh Corps was not likely to form the Porto Rico expedition. It was but partially organized, was deficient in drill, and inadequately equipped. Nor was Jacksonville at all a suitable place for the embarkation of an expedition. Its harbor was difficult of access, and of wholly insufficient depth to accommodate any, save a few of the lighter draft transports.

The following six weeks were spent in writing camp stories from Jacksonville, Tampa, Key West, and Miami, and in running down the many orders and rumors of orders for the forwarding of the expedition to Porto Rico. The days of June and the earlier days of July were probably more prolific than any others of the entire campaign in the production of rumors of projected advances of our army, and in the actual issue of orders for movement which were immediately followed by countermanding orders. It is somewhat doubtful if the War Department really knew what it wanted to do, or what it intended to do. The vociferous expressions and demands of a certain phase of journalism, and the outcry raised by congressmen and others whose enthusiasm ran beyond the boundaries of sound judgment, were far from being in harmony with the plans and wishes of the administration. Men of enthusiastic and sanguine temperament loudly asserted the ability of the United States to put hundreds of thousands of fighting men into the field, armed and equipped and ready for service, within a period which they measured by days. Men of sounder judgment, wider experience, and fuller knowledge, were well aware of the folly of such a proposition. Insistent demand for immediate movement sought to override impossibilities, and dire confusion was the inevitable result.

The situation, so far as the press and the public were concerned, was complicated by the circulation of "inside information," which may have been issued only as a "blind" to conceal genuine plans from interested Spanish observers, to whom a knowledge of our intentions would have been of incalculable service. An army of trained journalists and news-seekers was on the alert for possible clews that would guide them and their papers in the formation of plans for obtaining those accounts which must be furnished to their readers, and without which the journal would lose prestige as a source of the earliest and most accurate information. The Porto Rico expedition was a matter of less real moment, and was a much smaller affair, than the invasion of Cuba. Yet its despatch seemed to present even a greater tangle than did the larger enterprise. The unwisdom of any move on Havana during the early summer months became more and more apparent. The gradual development of the situation paved the way to the Santiago expedition. But there was nothing which made the immediate occupation of Porto Rico clearly imperative. The presence of the Cervera squadron in West Indian waters also arose as a restraining element.

The command, constitution, and the point of departure of the army for Porto Rico, remained open questions, and the newsboys who sold the papers were almost as accurately informed regarding the position as were the editors who printed them. Waiting correspondents telegraphed to their home offices, and the home offices replied to the waiting correspondents. The Porto Rico expedition was to leave Tampa on a certain day, and was to consist of the Fourth Corps, under General Coppinger. It was to start either from Miami or from Fernandina, and consist of the Seventh Corps, under General Coppinger. Again the rumor came that Lee was to start from Jacksonville with his command. Every major-general of the army who could not be otherwise accounted for, was assigned, by some more or less widely current report, to the command of the Porto Rican expedition. These various expeditions were formed, by these reports, of any and all troops having no other special destination. They were appointed to sail, by the same reports, upon various dates, and from a long list of Atlantic and Gulf ports. This is hardly an exaggeration, and it was from all this intricate maze of uncertain reports and rumors that correspondents and their chiefs were to extract the kernel of truth which would guide them in the way in which they should go.

At last, soon after the middle of July, everything appeared to focus around General Brooke and the First Army Corps. On the 19th, the following despatch reached me at Jacksonville: "Latest advices are General Brooke reaches Chickamauga to-morrow and then will decide what regiments leave with him for Porto Rico, with indications movement not begin before last this month. Fourth Corps said to be already embarked at Tampa."

The first part of this despatch was approximately accurate. The last part showed the effect of press censorship, which was very close at Tampa. Not a few of even the leading newspapers announced the departure of that Tampa expedition a number of days before the vessels left the wharves. On the following day, the 20th, a despatch came from the office, which read as follows:

"Best Washington advice is that you go to Newport News to embark."

Charleston had also come into prominence as the point from which the troops were to sail, and General Ernst's brigade of the First Corps was on its way to that port, with possibilities of being ordered to some other before reaching it. The Tampa detachment was in process of assembly. Even at so nearby a point as Jacksonville we were quite unable to learn either its composition or its probable day of sailing. We were told that it had gone, that it was to go, and that its orders had been countermanded, and that it would not go at all. General Miles had sailed, some days before, for Santiago, with more troops than were needed there, and was to proceed to Porto Rico with the surplus.

These four detachments, from Newport News, Charleston, Tampa, and Santiago, gradually assumed a definite shape, until there was no question that a force would move from each point. It became clearly evident that the Porto Rican invasion was to be the work, not of an army, but of an aggregation. In a force whose numerical strength was somewhat less than the half of an army corps, four different corps were represented. Brigades and regiments were detached from the commands with which they had been connected, and were assigned to this heterogeneous expedition in a way which, a little later, gave rise to serious conditions among the troops, by reason of the lack and derangement of the staff service which attends and provides for the line in the properly systematized organization. This undoubtedly was the main cause of the many serious difficulties encountered by our soldiers on the island of Porto Rico. Our military system provides for military organizations, with the corps, the division, the brigade, the regiment, and the company, as the descending sequence in the line of organization and supply, but it makes no adequate provision for miltiary conglomerations.

It became a problem of no easy solution to determine which of the three available detachments—Santiago being, of course, out of reach—presented the best combination of chances for interesting news-matter. Presumably, all would rendezvous at some previously determined point. But there was also the possibility that they would not. The result supported the possibility. The determination being left, in a measure, to my own judgment, I chose the Tampa detachment because it promised an early move which would put it in the fore-front in the days of the expected activity, and also because it was composed entirely of soldiers of our regular army, for which I confess to holding a very marked predilection. I therefore moved at once on Tampa.

Upon my arrival I found everything and everybody in a state of disorder and turmoil. The place was a bee-hive, an ant-hill, a toy-shop on Christmas-eve—anything that represents ceaseless activity and some apparent and some evident confusion. The expedition was on the eve of its departure, and everybody connected with it was saddled with a load which should have been distributed upon many shoulders. Eight transports were being loaded, two for Santiago and six for Porto Rico. Washington was telegraphing rush orders and trying to learn why a few men could not do the work which should have been apportioned among a hundred. The long wharf was crowded with stevedores, railroad men, officers, troopers, and civilians. Cars, loaded with supplies, were waiting the transference of their contents to the ships alongside. Artillery horses, cavalry horses, pack mules, ambulances and army wagons, stood in long lines, waiting to be rushed on board and stored as best they might be at the last moment.

It took several hours of tedious waiting before I could secure enough of the time of the overworked depot quartermaster to enable me to obtain the order which assigned me to a state-room on board the transport D. H. Miller. She was to carry my friends of Light Battery C of the Seventh United States Artillery. I desired to accompany them for personal reasons, and also for the hope that in those engagements which it was then supposed would form a part of the campaign, the artillery would be given its full measure of prominence. It was my wish to make a somewhat careful study of that rather neglected but highly important arm of our military service—the light field battery. As Battery C was equipped with the new pattern of gun using the smokeless powder, there appeared to be strong probability of its seeing active service if anybody did. We tried to get along without an adequate force of artillery at the battles before Santiago, and the plan is hardly to be credited with any marked degree of success.

Noon, on Saturday July 23d, saw four of the transports for Porto Rico on their way down the Bay of Tampa, with the other two to follow as soon as the inevitable "last things" could be done. General Miles had sailed from Santiago. General Ernst was on his way from Charleston, and General Brooke was getting ready with the detachment from Newport News. After months of waiting and weeks of make-believe preparation, the Porto Rican expedition had become a fact.

II

LIFE ON A TROOP-SHIP

Some Faults in Troop Transportation—Unnecessary Exposure to Danger—Soldiers Killing Time—Grumbling at the Commissary—Food of Officers and Privates—A Midnight Excitement—Encounter with the Eagle on the Blockading Line—Arrival at Ponce.

"To the front." Few words have a wider interest or a deeper meaning when the clarion of war has sounded in the ears of a nation. To the soldier who is to go, they mean the active service for which he has enlisted, the realization of his desires. They mean disappointment to those who stay behind in the camps. They mean care and pain and anxiety to hundreds of thousands of loving hearts at home. They are a text for a sermon and a title for a story. After months of routine work in camp, the bugle call of the "general," which is the signal for striking tents and loading baggage, comes as a welcome sound of sweet music to the soldier, if it follows orders which send the command "to the front." It is seldom that more than the briefest time is allowed for preparation. Farewell letters must be the work of such chance minutes as may be found free from other duties, and it often happens that such minutes do not come at all, and the soldier boy goes to the front with no "good-by" to the friends at home. Sometimes this is his fault, but more often it is an unfortunate result of his necessary duties.

Whether or no it be that all wars, and all campaigns and military expeditions present the same opportunities for criticism as does the Spanish-American entanglement of 1898, it is an unfortunate fact that few of the processes of the Porto Rico campaign are not open to severe criticism. It is difficult to deal with any of its phases without some censure for things done, and for others left undone. To omit this censure and the criticism, though neither is a pleasant feature to either the writer or the reader, would entail the exclusion from any story of the campaign of the summer of 1898 of very much that was among its prominent incidents and situations. The movement "to the front" of the Tampa detachment of the army for the invasion of Porto Rico presents its own set of incidents and conditions, which were far from being what they should have been.

The command was sent to sea, with no convoy, for a voyage of sixteen to eighteen hundred miles.

Probably, under the circumstances, a convoy would have been superfluous. The point is perhaps a minor one; but it was a military expedition, and the question of military form might be raised. But a more serious question was involved. An order, very vague and general, where it should have been definite and explicit, was issued, to the effect that the different vessels of the expedition should keep as near together as was practicable. At Cape Antonio a steamer, which we assumed to be the Arkadia, one of our consorts, showed faintly upon the horizon line some twenty miles to the southwest. The Whitney and the Florida were barely visible astern, while the Cherokee and the Mohawk, which were to start some hours behind us and overtake us through a superior speed, had not even shown their smoke. We lost them all, or they lost us, later on, and for several days we saw no one of them. We were thus, practically, an independent craft, running without reference to any others.

While we were doubtless wholly safe from any interference from Spanish or any other foreign vessels, we were not equally safe from the dangers of the sea, against which more careful and more ample provisions might and should have been made. We carried three hundred and thirty-five men, and one hundred and eighty horses. We carried four hundred and fifty rounds of ammunition for each of the six 3.2-inch field guns, besides the ammunition for a company of infantry. We had four boats and one life-raft. Not one of the boats would have lived in a heavy seaway, and one or two of them would hardly have floated on a mill-pond. Had any of the possibilities of an ocean voyage occurred, had fire broken out, or had we run into one of the hurricanes incident to that region, the soldiers of the United States would have been exposed to dangers and to risks which might have been greatly modified by the issuance of proper orders, which would have kept the ships within hailing distance of each other, or by the provision of an adequate equipment of boats and rafts.

As it was on the Miller, so it doubtless was on the other vessels. The men would smoke, and the utmost vigilance was required to keep them from smoking in the vicinity of the baled hay provided for the horses. It is true that our force on the Miller consisted of regulars, who are usually amenable to discipline. But it included a very large percentage of raw recruits, who had not learned that obedience is one of the principal requirements of a soldier's life. It was, therefore, the mercy of Providence, and not the wisdom or foresight of man, which kept that expedition from serious disaster. But all's well that ends well.

We were spared those dangers which were a constant possibility, and we sailed for days through the bluest of blue water, under the sunniest of sunny skies. The novelty of the voyage was exhausted during the first day out. Flying fishes lost their interest, and a school of porpoises ceased to be an excitement. The majority took to sleeping the hours away, though a few of the more energetic took to "nosey poker" and other games of cards. "Nosey poker" is a game which does not depend upon any recent visit of the army paymaster. The game is played by any number, and the loser, instead of giving up a portion of his thirteen dollars a month, is subjected to punishment for holding the weakest hand, by a fillip on the nose with the full pack of cards held, in turn, between the thumb and fingers of each of his opponents.

But sleeping was the popular occupation. The number of hours out of the twenty-four which some men can spend in sleep, day in and day out, is beyond the comprehension of any man who cannot catch a cat-nap during the day without paying for it by some hours of wakefulness during the following night. I have no reason to think that the men on board the D. H. Miller were endowed with any fuller measure of sleeping power than were the men on the other ships. What they did, I presume all to have done.

Scores of them slept all day, and then slept all night. They lay about the decks in all manner of conceivable and inconceivable attitudes and costumes. "Tattoo" and "taps" did not concern them. Few heard either, for long before the hour of their sounding, the decks, from bow to stern, were covered with the forms of sleeping men. There were bunks for them below, but the hard deck was chosen for its greater coolness.

Many complaints have been published of the sufferings of the soldiers on these transports. That they were subjected to various unavoidable physical discomforts is not to be denied. But the complaints would have come in any case, for the far greater portion of them came from the constitutional growlers. On many of the ships, the horses were the real sufferers. Therein lay an unfortunate mistake of our transportation department. There is no doubt that men can and will take care of themselves to very great extent. Horses cannot do this, and therefore should receive far more attention than was shown them on many of these vessels. This should be done, not only on the ground of mercy to dumb animals, but, as well, because these animals are indispensable in army service. The men cannot live in the field without the provisions which must be drawn to them by horses or mules; they cannot fight without the ammunition which must reach them by means of army wagons. Efficient service in battle depends almost entirely upon our four-footed servants, and they should be kept in the most of comfort and best of condition. This cannot be if they are stifled for ten days or two weeks on an ocean voyage.

From some of the pitiful tales which have been given space in some of our newspapers, concerning soldier-life on shipboard, one would be wholly justified in a conclusion that all hands spent the greater portion of their time enduring the agonies of slow starvation, while they listened to the popping of champagne corks, and the rattle of dishes laden with delicacies served for the delectation of the officers in the cabin. Naturally the officers did fare better than the men. But, in all complaints of this character, it is necessary to keep one fact clearly in mind, whether the complaint refer to conditions on ship-board or in camp. It is that the government feeds the private and the non-commissioned officer, while the commissioned officer has to feed himself. This he is free to do in any way which suits his taste and his pocket-book. If he wants champagne, he can have it by paying for it. If he wants strawberries in January, he can have them—by paying for them. If conditions be such that no market is available, the only way by which the officer may rightly and lawfully obtain the food which he needs, is by the purchase of rations from his command, or from some portion of it. For what he thus gets, he must pay a certain specified sum per day. The amount thus paid is applied to what is known as the "company fund," and may be expended, like the profits arising from the "canteen," for the benefit of the company mess.

This "company fund" is one of the channels through which the mess of the private in the regular army has an advantage over the mess of the volunteers. The government supply of three and a quarter pounds of food per day per man is above the average of individual consumption. Out of the daily supply for a company, the properly qualified cook easily effects a saving, and the surplus may be exchanged or sold for the benefit of the "company-fund." Through his wider experience, the regular has a better knowledge of the economy of resources, and thus holds an advantage over the less experienced volunteer. But the officers' mess is entirely their own affair, and is no more a matter for the comment or criticism of the privates than is the table of a railroad president a matter which concerns his employees. I have heard volunteer officers boast proudly that they "stayed with the boys," ate with them, and shared the details of their lives. I have never known a case of this kind in which the officer, through an undue familiarity with his men, did not materially and seriously weaken his influence over them. On board the transports, arrangements were made by which meals were served in the saloon to cabin passengers, officers, newspaper correspondents, or any other civilians who obtained government transportation. The usual price was fifty cents for each meal. On board the Miller this was collected daily. Whether the steward doubted our honesty or our financial resources, I am unable to say.

The Miller carried her full quota of the grumblers. One presented himself one day to complain to his commanding officer that the men were not receiving their due quantity of coffee. A few questions drew out the fact, already well known to the officer, that each man received a pint of coffee with each meal. He was sent away to digest his newly acquired information that the government supplied coffee for a beverage and not for bathing purposes. It is heavy odds that the next letter which that boy wrote to his home people made them long to send him a few pounds of Rio. Another complained that the coffee was ample in quantity, but was lamentably deficient in strength. There was nothing in either his appearance or his conversation to indicate that he was one who was accustomed to a pint of *café noir* three times a day, previous to his enlistment. Some complained that canned beans were served with undue frequency. Others wanted more beans. Some had too much canned beef and too little canned salmon. Others wanted less salmon and more beef. Some wanted a more frequent issue of canned tomatoes. Others did not want them at all.

The complainants were chiefly from the newly enlisted men, of which the commands on board contained an unusually large proportion. It was only possible to endeavor to show these men that it was out of the question for the government to try to run its commissary department on the European plan. Then they went away and wrote those pitiful tales of suffering, privation, and cruelty, which, in public press and in private letters, have added a wholly unwarranted fuel to the flame of public indignation against the shortcomings of the staff departments of the United States army. Men who, at home, would not think of going to a physician with their petty ailments, besieged the surgeon with doleful tales of aches and pains of which they showed no symptoms; and, because he measured their ailments at their true value, called him hard names behind his back and "wrote to the papers" about his neglect and indifference. A measure of excuse for some lies in the fact that it is very difficult to convince a man who is taking his first sea-voyage, that a mild touch of *mal de mer*, for which there is no remedy except getting over it, is not the early stages of some horrible and deadly disease.

But in spite of complaints and the fancied ailments of lives of utter idleness, nobody starved to death, and nobody died of sea-sickness. There was little to break the monotony. Occasional views of a distant coast became events. A close watch was kept for the vessels of our blockading fleet. An encounter with one of them led to an interesting conversation off the Isle of Pines, on the southern coast of Cuba, on the night of July 25th. The hour was midnight. The stars shone clearly overhead. Away to the northward vivid and frequent flashes of lightning outlined the heavy cloud masses which hung along the horizon. All on board the Decatur H. Miller were asleep, save those who were on duty. The decks were thickly strewn with the forms of sleeping soldiers, who found the decks a more comfortable dormitory than the hot and oppressive quarters provided for them below. The Miller was pounding her way through the surges of the Caribbean Sea at her usual pace of six knots an hour.

The conversation started with some sea-talk in the shape of a signal-light which gleamed from the darkness on the port quarter. An unknown something was out there telling the Miller to stop her engines. But the Miller kept on. The light shot forward, and from the dim, low-lying form on the surface of the water there came a flash and a report. That was another and a more emphatic way of saying "Stop!" It was treated as the light had been. Then the dark form showed three signal lights, one above the other, and ran up to within hailing distance, and the summons to "heave to" came through a megaphone. This produced the desired effect. The megaphone voice again came across the water, and it came in a tone that implied a very decided dissatisfaction with what had been done. Its tone was angry.

"What is the name of that ship?"

A less distinct megaphone replied from our pilot-house, "The D. H. Miller."

"What is the ship beyond you?"

"The Arkadia."

"Why did you not stop in answer to our signals?"

"I did not understand the signal."

"Why did you not stop when we fired?"

"I thought you might be a Spaniard."

"Have you soldiers on board?"

"Yes. Three hundred of them."

"Very well! Now I want to tell you that you are a natural born —— —— fool! You have endangered the life of every man on board your ship. If

I hadn't known that transports were coming, I should have filled you full of holes for not stopping when we fired. As for Spaniards, you need not be afraid of them. There is nothing on this coast that dare cross our lines, or even go outside the harbor. You will probably be stopped by five or six patrol-boats between here and Cape Cruz. You need not worry about any Spaniards, but when anything out here tells you to stop, YOU STOP! Now go ahead, and good luck to you all."

This little speech may have been lacking in punctilio and in those lines of fine courtesy which are a marked characteristic of the officers of our navy, but it was a marvel of directness, force, lucidity, and truth. Its meaning was as clear as the day. It was answered by a burst of hearty applause and cheers from the men who thronged the sides of the Miller. Three rousing cheers came from the little gun-boat, which proved to be the saucy and nervy Eagle, one of the most dashing and successful boats on the blockading line. Then the signal-lights went out and the dusky shape slid away into the darkness toward the coast.

It was quite an episode. The men lay awake on the deck discussing it, and we of the cabin sat in pajamas, night-shirts, and underwear, for a review of the situation. We pronounced our ship captain to be guilty of high crime and misdemeanor. The ranking military officer on board was authorized to visit the captain of the ship, and announce our sentence that he be keel-hauled, mast-headed, and then hung at the yard-arm, if such a contrivance could be found on board the steamer. The officer, hatless, barefooted, and clad only in undignified and unofficial underwear, proceeded on his fearful errand. But, upon his arrival, he evidently exercised the authority with which he was vested by reason of his official position, and modified the sentence. He proceeded to say things in a manner which may be learned at West Point, though the form is not included in the prescribed studies of that institution. From the sulphurous smell which was wafted through the cabin windows during the next few minutes, it was quite clear to the rest of us that the captain of Company F, Eleventh United States Infantry, was doing his duty like a man—and a sinner. Within those minutes, the captain of the Miller gained some valuable information with regard to the wisdom and safety of monkeying with the vessels of the United States Navy.

We were obliged to stop at Daiquiri, on the Cuban coast, and again at Samana Bay, on the coast of San Domingo, to obtain supplies of water for the horses. We had sailed under sealed orders which, when opened, gave us instructions to proceed to Fajardo, the northeastern point of Porto Rico. As we left the bay of Samana, we were met by the United States gun-boat Annapolis, which had been sent out to intercept the arriving transports, and to give orders for their procedure to Ponce, on the south coast of the island. They gave us news of the landing at Guanica of the detachment from Santiago, under command of General Miles. They also told us of the surrender of Ponce without a shot. On the night of August 2d, we dropped anchor off the harbor of Ponce, and waited for daylight and a pilot to take our ship to an anchorage among the fleet of transports and warships which had arrived before us.

III

EARLY DAYS ON THE ISLAND

Porto Rico or Puerto Rico—The Carib Title—Boriquén—First Impressions of the Island—The Harbor of Ponce—Unloading Transports—Soldiers as Stevedores—Mutual Curiosity—La Playa—The City of Ponce—Appearance of the Common People—Pedlers—The Island Ponies—Shopping Experiences—Courtesy from a Citizen.

THE little spot in the tropical seas, which we know as Porto Rico, has had a somewhat peculiar experience in the matter of its nomenclature. Throughout much the greater parts of its history it has either borne a nickname or a name which did not at all belong to it. Even its old Carib title has been a point of more or less contention among historians.

Dr. Chanca, writing in the year 1493, calls it Buriquén. Pedro Mártir de Anglería, in 1494, calls it Burichena. Juan de la Cosa, in 1500, calls it Boriquén. A writer in 1517 drops back to Buriquén. From the years 1535 to 1647 the form of Boriquén was adopted by the leading writers and historians. In 1788, Fray Inigo Abbad, one of the leading authorities on the history of the island, turns it into

Borínquen, a form of doubtful correctness, but that which is most commonly used to-day by the island people. On nearly all of the maps of the island, its northwest corner is indicated under the title of Cape Borínquen. Borínquen is the spelling usually adopted by the local press, and a number of stores in different cities display the sign of "La Borinquéna." Later writers, among them Washington Irving and Emilio Castelar, use the apparently better authorized Boriquén, while Otto Neussel, in 1892, gives it Burinquén. Others have given it Burenquén, Boricua, Burikem, Burinkem, Borichen, and some have simply called it Bo. Some early writers mention it as "La Isla de Carib."

An effort has been made to determine the meaning of the name by a philological process, with results which seem eminently plausible. By dividing the word into three syllables, Bo-ri-quén, and translating them through comparison with the same syllables where they occur in words whose meaning is known, a Porto Rican authority, Sr. Dr. Cayetano Coll y Toste, gives the meaning as "Tierra del Valiente Señor," or practically, "The Land of the Valiant Lord." Dr. Coll's arguments appear to be reasonably exhaustive, and probably the majority of American people will be quite ready to accept his conclusions without any argument.

Disposing of the tangle in the Carib name of the island, we immediately run into another in its Spanish title. When el Almirante Cristóbal Colón, whose name we have twisted into Christopher Columbus, discovered the island of Boriquén, on his second voyage, he gave it the name of San Juan Bautista (St. John the Baptist), in honor of the familiar figure of New Testament history. This name was applied to the island and not to a city on its coast. In a letter, dated November 14, 1509, from the King of Spain to el Almirante don Diego, son of Cristóbal, reference is twice made to "la isla de San Juan," "the island of San Juan."

A city, which we now know as San Juan, situated upon the shore of a beautiful harbor on the northern coast, received the name of Puerto Rico (rich port). In process of time the city became San Juan de Puerto Rico, there came a confounding of the terms, and the whole island became a "rich port," or harbor, which is not at all a fitting name for its general coast line.

For our use of the name "Porto" Rico there is no authority, save its establishment by common usage in this country. In spite of its general establishment, it is unquestionably a corrupt term, with no adequate warrant for its adoption. It is a compounding of the Spanish *rico* with the Portuguese *porto*. The

United States Transports off Port Ponce.

Board of Geographic Names decided during Harrison's administration in favor of Puerto Rico. The Post-office Department has adopted Porto Rico. The Navy Department is said to favor Puerto Rico, and when General Miles in his recent report used the latter spelling, the Government Printing Office changed it to Porto.

Any radical change in the name of the island might be difficult of accomplishment. It would involve a universal as well as a national and local change.

But as we have expelled those who, by a derangement of names of their own application, have given the island an inappropriate title, it might not be a bad idea for us to return to them the name "Puerto Rico," and christen the island with the long-disused and historic and fitting title of Boriquén. No doubt the northeast trade-winds have blown as refreshingly over Puerto Rico as they would have blown over San Juan Bautista. The coffee and the sugar-cane, the banana and the cocoa-nut, have flourished in Puerto Rico. They would undoubtedly grow quite as luxuriantly in the territory and potential state of Boriquén.

The opening days of the month of August, 1898, saw busy times in the city and harbor of Ponce. The place had become ours almost without our asking for it. This southern gateway of the island of Porto Rico had been thrown open to our army, and the people of the city had met us with the hand-clasp of a cordial welcome. For many years they had felt that they were being bowed down and crushed under the heavy hand of an oppressor. The army of the United States was regarded as the sword-bearing hand of a deliverer who, in the coming days, would lay aside the sword, and wield, in its place, the horn of plenty, scattering peace, riches, and blessings throughout the sun-kissed island. It was an armed and warlike force which landed there in Ponce, but, in the city itself, there was no use for weapons.

The first impression of the vicinity is a pleasant one, even aside from the fact that almost any land looks pleasant after one has spent a week or two at sea. The picture offered by the approach is strongly attractive. The bay itself is a pretty one, though as a harbor it is somewhat treacherous. Three or four miles back from the coast, to the northward, a line of hills of from one to two thousand feet in height makes a picturesque sky-line. Southward lie the waters of the Caribbean Sea. To the eastward the land lies an almost level swamp and plain, covered with a dense growth of tropical plants and foliage. Just westward of the port the shore trends southward in a graceful curve, its line fringed with cocoa-nut trees and rich verdure, and rising almost immediately to low hills, and from them to the higher range beyond. The continuation of this curve, to the westward, forms the bay of Ponce. Seaward from the ends of the arc thus formed are a few straggling islands and reefs, which are wholly or partly covered at high water. On one of these islands off the eastern point stands a light-house. The water of the bay shoals gradually, so much so that the lighters upon which the troops, horses, and cargoes were transferred from the ships to shore, were propelled by long poles, even from vessels which lay half a mile from the miniature apologies for wharves which skirt the shore in front of the custom-house.

In the harbor and on the shore all was bustling activity, as the Miller came to anchor in the inner bay. Warships, transports, press-boats, and colliers, lay in close proximity to each other. Steam launches, naphtha launches, sail-boats, and row-boats, wound in and out among them, carrying passengers and messages from ship to ship, or between ship and shore. Unwieldy lighters loaded with horses, mules, supplies, and all the impedimenta of a moving army, were poled through the shallow water to the shore by dark-skinned boatmen in scanty raiment. On shore, the confusion was even greater than that on water. The absence of system and the lack of departmental organization were manifest everywhere. Piles of stores and equipments lined the narrow beach. Sheds were being erected upon the quay to cover the great heaps of forage and rations which had been put ashore there. Soldiers and civilians thronged the narrow streets. Officers of arriving troops did not know where to go with their commands, and there was no one to direct them. Reporting their arrival at headquarters, they were simply told to get their men and supplies on shore as best they could, to find a camping ground somewhere, and to get into camp as soon as possible. Of order, system, or organization, there was no sign.

A naval officer from the Columbia had been appointed harbor-master, and it was only his cool head and quick judgment that kept matters from utter chaos. Of competent military staff organization there was nothing. There was no depot quartermaster, no depot commissary, no hospital service. Had we, on landing, encountered a hostile force, as there was some reason for thinking we should, the landing at Santiago would have been duplicated in all its disorder, with all its entailed miseries. With weeks of time for preparation, the force sent for the invasion of Porto Rico was a collection of troops, and not an organization. It was a conglomeration, and not an army. Those early days in Ponce showed,

A Typical Street in Port Ponce.

EARLY DAYS ON THE ISLAND 33

very clearly, one of two things: Either our system is not sufficiently elastic, or it is folly to form an army of invasion by the assembling of small detachments from different organizations. In theory, the line is the fighting force for which the staff provides, and to which it supplies food, clothing, ammunition, tentage, and transportation. The staff is supposed to provide for the line, whether it be in camp or in the field. Weakness in the staff, means weakness in the line. Confusion in the staff, means confusion in the line. As things were managed there in those early days of the campaign, it is wholly well for us that our soldiers had so little fighting to do.

For the transfer to the shore, the soldiers were turned into stevedores and 'longshoremen. The officers of the American army are not generally trained to the business of handling and forwarding merchandise, of acting as head-stevedores, and of serving as captains of harbor-lighters; but, with the American adaptability to circumstances, they found a way to get load after load to the shore to be piled there by details from their commands, to await removal to the camp. The removal was a simpler process than the unloading. The army wagons accompanying the different commands were reinforced by hundreds of the native bullock teams. The army wagon is the more rapid method of transportation, but the Porto Rican bullock-driver gets a fair amount of speed out of his team by the active use of a very long-handled goad and a judicious indulgence in Porto Rican profanity. Those were busy days and profitable for the laborers and teamsters of Ponce.

They were interesting days for all the people of the place. Large horses were not wholly a novelty to them, but large horses by the hundreds was something which they had never seen before. The people stood in crowds, with open mouths and staring eyes to see load after load of our big army horses and mules brought ashore by the lighters. Our tall and brawny soldiers were a type of men which they did not know. Our field-guns were new to them. The tons upon tons of supplies gave them a wholly new idea of national resources. The interest and the curiosity were far from being one-sided. To all save a few of the Americans, our new people and their ways, their little horses, and the products of the country, were as new and strange and interesting, as we and our ways were to them. For many days the port city of Ponce, known as La Playa—"the shore"—was a swarming centre into which were poured men by the thousand, and merchandise and munitions of war by the hundreds of tons, to wait a few brief hours until the men could be got

EARLY DAYS ON THE ISLAND 35

into their camps, and the materials distributed to their proper places.

Although my work took me constantly back into it all, it was an endless relief to get away from this headless hurly-burly, and into the comparative quiet of an army camp. This also gave one a chance to look about a bit, and see what manner of land it was to which we had come. Ponce is a sort of compound place. It consists of the city proper, some two miles inland; and of the port city, La Playa, immediately upon the shore. The port city consists of a half-dozen streets running parallel with the shore, east and west, crossed at right angles by another set, Philadelphia fashion, though they are on a much smaller scale in every way. The streets are from twenty to thirty feet in width, with sidewalks, where there are any at all, of about three feet.

The buildings are chiefly commercial warehouses, used for storage purposes in connection with foreign trade. With few exceptions they are of a single story in height, built of rough masonry faced with mortar, which has scaled off in many places, revealing the rough structure of the walls. The buildings are windowless, the openings being provided with iron or wooden shutters. To the east and to the west of the body of the city are small wooden dwellings, most of them of cheap construction, and few of them appearing to be other than the homes of the laborers about the harbor. A few blocks to the northeast of the custom-house, which appears to be the focal point of the port city, stands a church, very Spanish in architecture and appearance, and much in need of paint and repairs.

The city proper seems to be a place very well worth possessing. So distinctly favorable were my impressions after spending a few days in Ponce, that I was almost tempted to modify my views on the subject of territorial expansion. The city lies pleasantly, and is pleasant in itself. It bears no resemblance to any American city. Its streets are narrow, and its buildings which exceed two stories in height are few in number. The cleanliness of its streets was a pleasing surprise, and the prevailing tints of gray and pale blue, mingled with the green of the shade-trees of the park and the court-yards of private residences, give to the whole place an atmosphere of pleasant coolness. With the blue sky and bright sunshine the city is decidedly attractive, and one in search of a pleasant home might easily go farther and fare worse.

Approaching the city from the coast, one passes over two miles of an excellent macadam road kept in very fair condition. It connects the city proper with its port city on the immediate sea-coast. Along the

A Street Scene in Port Ponce.

way one sees the rude shack of the negro, the home of modest comfort, and the villas, which are evidently occupied by citizens of fair income. There are several large fields of sugar-cane, one or two sugar mills, an ice plant, and a Protestant church, the only one on the island. In the heart of the city there is a well-kept park, which occupies about the same area as an ordinary New York city block. It has shade-trees, walks, and flower-beds. In the centre there is a large pavilion of Moorish architecture. Adjoining the park stands the cathedral, conventional in architecture and weather-beaten in appearance. Stores and residences, with the central or rear court-yard with their trees and shrubs, face the square and the cathedral.

The arrangement of the streets of Ponce is, generally, that of the parallelogram. They are all well metalled, and most of them appear to be well kept. In case of excessive dust, as a result of drought, it would be quite easy to obtain a supply of water from the hills by gravity pressure, which could be used for street-sprinkling. The place claims three hotels, though one who is at all familiar with American hostelries is somewhat loath to apply the name of hotel to such establishments as those at Ponce. One gets a place to sleep, food to eat, and a bottle of wine, all at reasonable prices.

It is anybody's guess whether the American soldiers or the Porto Rico people derived the greater amount of entertainment from new scenes and unfamiliar experiences in our newly acquired territory. The Ponce road, which covers the two miles of distance between the city and the port of Ponce, was an endless panorama of life and movement. The points at either end of the road swarmed with people riding, driving, walking; with army-wagons and native ox-carts; with squads and troops of soldiers, mounted and on foot. The procession began almost with the early morning "reveille," and lessened, though it did not cease, only with the notes of "retreat" at sunset. Back and forth, between the port and the city, and the camps beyond the city, moved two mingling currents, going in opposite directions.

The native spectator was astonished not only by the vast number of heavy horses and mules used by the army, but by the great wagons piled high with their loads of camp supplies and equipment, and by the score or more of ships in the harbor, from whose capacious holds and between-decks the numerous fleet of lighters transported to the shore a seemingly endless amount of material for subsistence and for warfare. It was a wholly unfamiliar scene to all except the very few who had crossed the water to some large city of Europe or America. It was, in its way, as I have intimated, an object-lesson in national wealth and national resources, and will leave its impression deeply marked upon the minds of our new citizens. The Americans stared at the people and their ways of life, which were new and strange to them.

The common people of the island are a mixture of all shades of color, from full black to yellow, with here and there a paler tint. Comfort and economy appear to be the chief ends to be served in the matter of wearing apparel. Neither style nor cleanliness seems to be of any consideration with the masses. Many men and women are barefooted, and many a dusky-skinned toddler of four or five years and under is wholly free from any fear of soiling his or her pinafore, by reason of being wholly free from the pinafore—or anything else. Masculine apparel usually consists of a battered hat, a cotton shirt, cotton trousers, and shoes—sometimes. Feminine apparel is a matter for feminine description and feminine ears. I only know that, among the class to which I am now referring, the feminine portion looks very baggy, very slouchy, and, usually, very dirty. Men, women, and children appear to occupy the bulk of their time in eating mangoes, that fruit which Lady Brassey so aptly describes by pronouncing it to be one of the most delicious of fruits, but to be eaten only in one's bath-tub.

When not busy eating mangoes, scores of these people parade the streets and the Ponce roads in search of wealth. The street-pedler is quite a feature in the cities of the island, but their number and their activity was vastly augmented by the influx of so large a number of possible customers. They peddled mangoes, cocoa-nuts, and other fruits, and a variety of indescribable pastes in which cocoanut appeared to be the chief ingredient. Many of these were quite toothsome and would be wholly enjoyable if one could but feel any sort of reasonable assurance with regard to the conditions under which the stuff is manufactured. Feeling it to be my duty to investigate all local conditions as closely as possible, I experimented with every kind of fruit, paste, confection, and compound, solid or liquid, offered for consumption and guaranteed to be of local production or manufacture.

I think that the most generally satisfactory experiment which I tried was the local ice-cream served after the manner of that variety known in America as the "hoky-poky." A dusky damsel, clad in none too abundant and not over-immaculate raiment, intimated in sign language, backed by a pleasant smile and the word "dos," which, under such circumstances does not mean two centavos, but two articles or measures for one centavo, that it would be her pleas-

Main Road, Ponce to Port Ponce.

ure to serve the "Americano." Not wishing to die alone, if death lay in the cup, I invited a group of soldier-men who stood by to risk their lives with me in an experiment on the material. I think there were ten of them, and I treated the whole crowd for the sum of seven cents, in our money. But I was quite agreeably disappointed. The compound appeared to be nothing more than frozen cocoa-nut milk slightly sweetened. I recommend it. It offers great possibilities in the hands of an artist. I think less highly of the local mango. It has a distinct flavor of turpentine, and the fibre of its pulp, getting immovably fixed between one's teeth, is far too greatly conducive to profanity.

Along this main road and about the streets of either of the terminal cities one sees scores and scores of the little, scrawny, island ponies, hardly larger than good-sized rocking-horses, gaunt, bony, and pitiful, with their fruit-filled basket-work panniers surmounted by the proprietor of the outfit, who rides in much the attitude of one sitting on a chair, with his bare feet hanging in front of the horse's chest, and flapping about with every step which the animal takes. Some of the women and children carry baskets of fruit or of the fruit paste, while others carry their wares in trays borne on the top of the head. Two-seated carriages, drawn by the sorriest, most scrubby and bony little horses imaginable, thread their more rapid way by a serpentine course in and out through the slowly moving throng of wagons and carts. One cannot help feeling sorry for these poor brutes of hack ponies, though as their structure seems to consist entirely of skin and bone, the constant and almost rhythmical movement of the driver's whip appears to have but little effect upon them. That whip movement is almost as methodical as the stroke of the piston of a Corliss engine. But the horses do not seem to mind it, and most of us are unable to deliver a lecture, in Spanish, on the subject of cruelty to animals. There is work in our new land for the S. P. C. A.

The legal fare between the city and the port is fixed, I believe, at twelve and a-half cents, Porto Rico money. But the only Americans who get out of it for any such figure are the lucky and the assertive who are willing to haggle or battle for their rights. If one be sweet-tempered and philosophical, he can obtain an endless amount of entertainment in essaying some commercial transaction with the local merchants. I wanted a rubber blanket. Rubber blankets do not seem to be a common article in Ponce. I visited some twenty or thirty stores. Half of them displayed the sign of "English Spoken." I found no difference between those and the others. I began my researches by a distinct enunciation of "I want a rubber blanket." This invariably produced something white. Sometimes it was white duck trousers, sometimes a shirt or collar. My "blanket" was supposed to be my best shot at "blanco" (white). I then tried "poncho," which I supposed to be a Spanish word. This was wholly unintelligible. "Poncho" is a purely South American term. I then fell back on sign language. For two hours I went through this process. I tried words and then gymnastics. I put my muscular system through a series of antics and contortions that, in America, would either have landed me in a lunatic asylum or a circus. I got everything but the thing I wanted. The range of articles offered in response to my gibbering and my antics extended from a mackintosh to a box of sardines. I failed to see where the sardines came in.

I visited stores of various kinds, and found them well supplied with the merchandise of their different lines, the stock neatly kept and well displayed. The goods were the manufacture of different nations, a few American, some French, English, and German. Spain was unduly represented, through the operation of tariff laws which were distinctly in favor of that country. Prices were probably not unreasonable, considering the cost of freight and the exorbitant duty. Flour, on which there is a high tariff, was quoted at thirty to thirty-five cents per pound in Porto Rico money, equivalent to one-half of that amount in our money. The campaign hat which I wore, and for which I paid $1 in Chattanooga, I was told would sell for $3.50, Porto Rico money, in Ponce. I was wearing a brown canvas shooting-coat for which I paid $1.50 in Jacksonville. I was told that the same sum would not even purchase the cloth to make it in Ponce. Ice is quoted at about the same price as that in most of our Southern cities where ice is manufactured. On cigars I thought I did quite well. I called for such a cigar as was used by the general run of smokers. I received a very fair article of the weed, free smoking and agreeable in flavor, made from native tobacco. I am not an expert in "twofers," but I have often paid a dime for a less satisfactory cigar than those for which I paid the equivalent of $2 per hundred, American money, in Ponce.

There is no doubt that we were welcome visitors in those days, though we have somewhat modified the heartiness with which we were received, through situations some of which could, while others could not, have been avoided. At that time I saw no scowls, Scores of men who, from their dress and bearing, were evidently of the best class of citizens, bowed, smiled, and saluted. There was no subservience, only marked courtesy and cordial hospitality. I wanted some nisperos. The merchant to whom I applied had none, but he summoned a messenger to guide me to a private residence a third of a mile away where I could get them fresh from the trees. The place, which had once been a fine one, was somewhat gone to decay, but the courteous gentleman who owned it welcomed me and sent for chairs to be placed for us in the cool shade of a huge mango-tree. The señora joined us, and a small black-skinned urchin was sent to gather the fruit I wanted. Naked and half-naked children, apparently belonging to the colored servants, played about us in company with three or four puppies.

I tendered pay for the fruit. It was refused, and I was told in the old form of Spanish hospitality that the fruit was mine, the trees on which it grew were mine, the house was mine, and its proprietor my most obedient servant. I fancy that he would make a good effort to hang on to his real estate if I had accepted his statement in strict literalness, but I was better off by more nisperos than I could carry. The gentleman's satisfaction with the new condition was quiet, but it was evidently honest and earnest. It was less vociferous than that displayed by our waiter in a café where another citizen was asked his feeling in the matter of the change of affairs. The waiter overheard the question, and quite brought down the house by his vigorous howl of " *Viva los Americanos.*" But the same sentiment appeared to pervade all classes. A local paper changed its title to *La Nueva Era. Ano I. Número I.* (The New Era. Year I. Number I.)

IV

THE CITY OF PONCE

Our Reception—Busy Days—Two Centres of Activity—Amusements—Police Department—Fire Department—The Market—Ponce Stores—A Lesson in Spanish.

WE went to Porto Rico expecting battles. We arrived there and were invited to receptions. It was a somewhat incongruous situation, with a side which savored of the opera bouffe. Such of our enemies as had been stationed in the vicinity of our landing, made a hasty and undignified exit, with only an occasional shot as they ran. The people bade us welcome, hung out American flags, and called down the blessings of Heaven upon our heads. Like all invading armies, we had carried with us a very large spirit of belligerency. We were much puzzled to know what to do with it when we got to Porto Rico. A portion of it was kept alive for the resistance which was anticipated as the army moved northward across the island. The rest of it became transmuted into sociability with a people who, immediately upon our arrival, pronounced themselves Americans, and gave their address as Porto Rico, U. S. A.

For the first two weeks everything was in a state of turmoil, but there were two strongly marked centres of activity. One of these was the custom-house at the shore city; the other the Hotel Français in the city proper. The custom-house served not only for its special purpose, but became, as well, the military head-quarters, the United States post-office, the telegraph station, and the place where everybody went to find out a great deal which could not be learned there. Transports arrived almost daily, bringing more troops and more supplies and more confusion. Plans were being formulated for the continuance of the campaign, and such troops as were designated for immediate participation in it, were moved forward as rapidly as possible. The rest were sent into camp in the vicinity of the city.

To those who find pleasure in the study of crowds, La Playa was a rich and profitable field. The crowd was not of the dense variety. It was rather a throng, active, restless, ebullient. Soldiers, civilians, and laborers moved uneasily about, some in idle curiosity, some seeking for a particular person or place, but the majority busily engaged in the piling up or the removal of forage, rations, and supplies. Every available native laborer was set to doing something.

Army officers bustled about superintending the transfer of the men and materials belonging to their commands. Naval officers sauntered about clad in immaculate white duck. There was an infinity of detail, but the general impression left upon the mind of the observer, was only that of a kaleidoscope in which the bits of color were men in uniform, horses, cannons, and boxes of hardtack and canned goods, with the blue water of the bay for a background.

The streets were a seemingly inextricable jumble of army wagons, carriages, and bullock-teams. The rumble and rattle of the slowly moving train was punctuated frequently by the shouts of the bullock drivers, and occasionally by the compliments paid in emphatic American by some driver of a heavily loaded army wagon, to some unfortunate goad-wielder or hack-driver who blocked his passage. That the anathemas were not understood by those on whose heads they fell, made no shadow of difference. Their import was fully realized, and they usually proved quite effective.

A secondary focus of activity at the Playa was found in an establishment wherein one could obtain a wide variety of forms of liquid refreshment. I was told that before the arrival of the Americans, the place was on the very verge of bankruptcy. A week later, the proprietor was reckoned among the financially solid men of the place. Naturally, more or less of our men overdid matters in their efforts to find the most cooling and refreshing compound. It became necessary to issue a military order prohibiting the sale of intoxicants to soldiers. The order was, of course, obeyed, but it is always a remarkable fact that many men can be overcome by non-alcoholic compounds, or by alcoholic compounds sold under some other name. A guard-house was established in one corner of the custom-house, and it was seldom without guests.

At the uptown centre, the throng was almost equally active, though its interests were of different character. The Playa was the centre of industry. The Hotel Français was the centre of recreation and sociability. The Playa was the official military head-quarters. The hotel was the head-quarters of the newspaper correspondents, and the resort for army and naval officers off duty. It was a quaint old place with nothing at all to recommend it particularly as a hotel under ordinary conditions. Its dungeon-like closets in which its guests were supposed to sleep, must have furnished infinitely more satisfaction to the fleas and mosquitoes than they did to those who furnished feeding-grounds for those insects. The stone-paved coffee-room with its one long table, was attractive to those who frequented it, rather by reason of what they themselves brought to it than because of what was served upon it.

That room was often the scene of honest and hearty joviality. Its frequenters were men who had seen something, and had something to say about what they had seen. Some had been through the Santiago campaign as observers, and some had taken part in it. Correspondents were there who had spent weeks on despatch-boats, and naval officers were there who had spent weeks on the blockade. Army officers, both line and staff men, were there to tell of their experiences. Many a man will remember those days with pleasure. There was much drinking, but it was of a mild type, and pre-eminently social in its nature. Lemonade and claret-cup were the popular refreshments, and the heavier fluids found but little demand. The local prices were seriously affected. Lemonade was served in flagons. For the first few days this cost ten centavos the flagon. Then the price went up, and it cost ten centavos for each glass served from the flagon. Mineral water rose to forty centavos the pint bottle, and the attendants grew very keen for tips.

The hotel was the news-centre. All was told there that the various news-gatherers had to tell. Those who had driven out to the "firing-line," to "*El* front," as it was facetiously called, on the previous day, told of their observations at that position. Those who had been to head-quarters at the Playa, told of what was to be heard there. Army movements and processes were subjects of comment and criticism. The probability of an early peace and the chances of recall were topics of profound interest to many. The evening dinner was a time of good-natured uproar and clamor. The house was overcrowded, its service and facilities were inadequate for the multitude which besieged it. Unless one came sharply upon the hour for the opening of the dining-room, it was well for him if he brought no very eager appetite with him.

Under ordinary circumstances I should set Ponce down as a disappointing place to visiting strangers, until they had made the acquaintance of some of those charming people who make the city their home. Its surroundings are undeniably attractive, but the stranger finds a dearth of entertainment in the city itself. The place claims a population of between twenty and thirty thousand in the city proper, with jurisdiction over a surrounding territory the inclusion of which leads to the occasional publication of figures ranging from forty to forty-five thousand as the population of the city of Ponce. The conditions which existed during my visit to the place were, of course, abnormal. It was, therefore, not

A Street in Ponce.

easy to note the usual resources in the matters of entertainment and interest for either the people of the city or for those who might visit it.

The theatre, called La Perla—the Pearl—is a structure of some pretensions, in which performances are given from time to time by such companies of theatrical or opera people as may appear. Most of these come out from Spain, and make the tour of the West Indies. Local talent also appears in occasional performances. The building is chiefly of iron and marble, and its cost is said to have exceeded 70,000 pesos. Adjoining the theatre is a large and well-equipped Casino, or club-house. There are various minor clubs and organizations, and one or two theatres of inferior character. Aside from these it is not easy to see just what society in Ponce does to amuse itself outside of private social functions. In common with very many of the Spanish-American cities, there is the Sunday night promenade on the plaza. This occurs to some extent during the week, but Sunday night the attendance is larger and more attention is paid to dress. It becomes a sort of dress parade for the better class of people. The band plays, and the throng moves back and forth, up and down, up and down, the length of the plaza. Others sit in rented chairs along the sides and ends, and watch them as they walk. To me it seemed a kind of social treadmill; though I could readily see how it might have become—as it probably was a recognized meeting-place—a sort of general public reception at which everyone met everyone else, with the opportunity for a chat if it was wished, a dignified bow, or a cold shoulder.

Ponce had a police department. It appeared to be composed chiefly of good-looking young fellows who wore a uniform and carried a sword. They seemed to be a mild, inoffensive lot, and presented no special evidence of power to quell a riot or to handle an exciting election. It is doubtful if they see much service in either of those lines. The Porto Ricans are not a turbulent race, nor are they given to intoxication and nocturnal disturbances. I could see but little use for the police at all. I did see one stop a horse who was trotting up the street after having capsized the cart to which he was attached, in turning a corner too sharply. I also saw one of these limbs of the law shake his head sadly as he watched an intoxicated countryman ride unsteadily along the way, shouting "Viva Puerto Rico." I saw another risk his life in expostulating with two street pedlers who were discussing, with some animation, their individual rights to occupy a certain shady corner. A New York "copper" would have made them "move on," or would have collared both of them and taken them to the station-house on a charge of disorderly conduct.

Ponce has a fire department which consists of an old-fashioned "tub" hook and ladder truck, and a couple of hose-reels. These are housed in a flamboyantly decorated structure in the rear of the cathedral, which gives it a facing on the principal street. The firemen wear flaming red shirts, a very broad belt, and dark trousers. They have very little to do except to draw their pay and stand around looking as if they were extremely useful. From the presence of a bugler among their number, I infer that their orders when in action are sounded upon the bugle instead of roared unintelligibly through a brass trumpet or other medium. The old-fashioned brass trumpet would seem more in keeping with the general outfit of the Ponce fire department, but the penetrating cry of the bugle really does seem better adapted for the purpose for which it is used. The swarm of these red-shirted fire-fighters, which is in over-ample evidence at performances in the theatre, suggests, almost too plainly, that there is need for their presence. This is not the fact, probably, but their presence in such number brings up the idea. The water-supply of the city is obtained by gravity pressure from a stream in the hills, and it would seem as though a readjustment of the fire department might be effected with a considerable economy to the city treasury.

The market is doubtless fully up to the requirements of the place, but it was far behind that of Mayaguez, though the latter is a less populous city. Doubtless also the local way of getting supplies for the table is wholly satisfactory to the people, but it was lacking in many features which Americans find convenient and desirable. The market opens at some unearthly hour in the morning. I never spent a night there to note the hour at which the first arrival put in his appearance. I did stop there one morning on my way to San Juan, to get a cup of coffee. It was four o'clock and pitch dark, but the coffee was there, hot and strong. So were at least fifty or seventy-five people. I could not see how many might be out in the darkness beyond, but there were those in the immediate vicinity of the coffee-stands. All the way along the road, for the first ten miles of our journey that morning, we met the people coming in with their little stock of garden products to be exposed for sale. How early the buyers turn out, I do not know, but the sellers are certainly of the "early bird" variety.

A brief acquaintance with the Ponce market would lead the average observer to a conclusion that it was a poor man's institution. The same will hold true

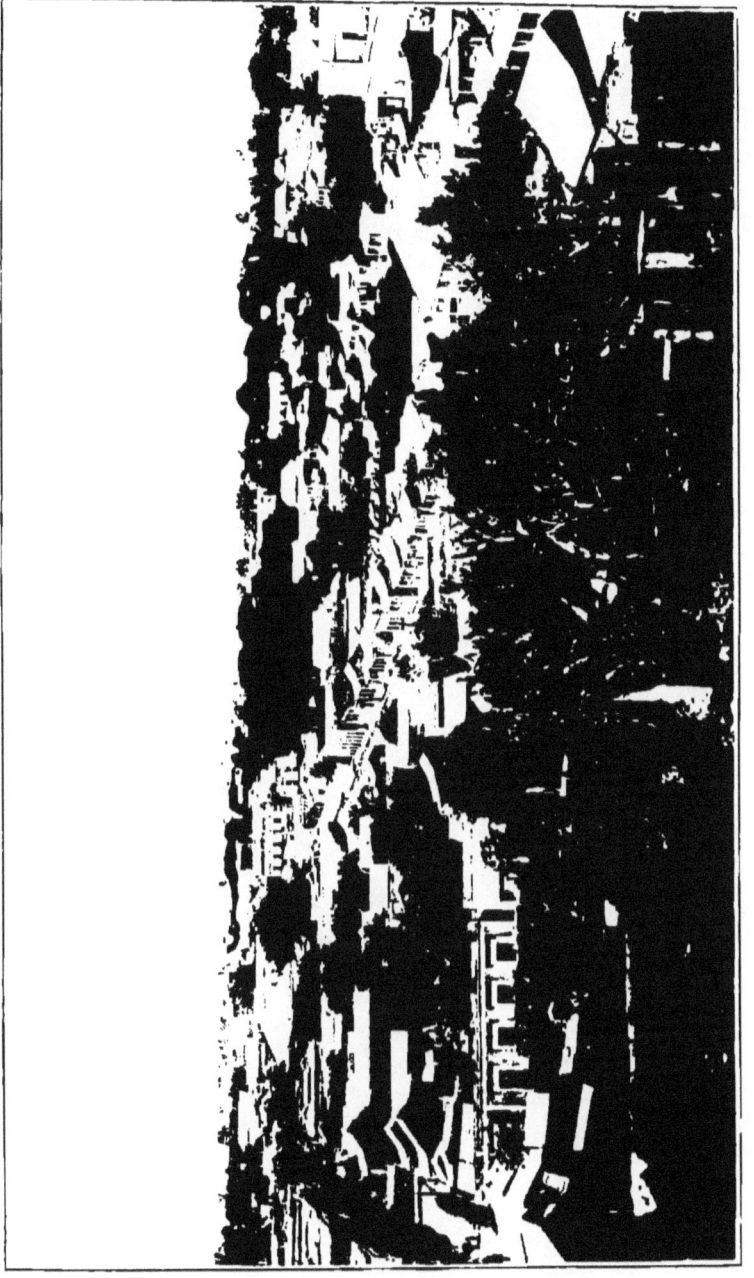

View of Ponce from the Hospital.

of all the city markets of Porto Rico. One rarely sees a well-dressed buyer. All seem to be of the poorer classes, and the smallness of their purchases seems to indicate a necessity for economy. Many of them, however, are the servants of the people of the better class, doing the daily marketing for the family by which they are employed. One of the noticeable features of all these island cities and towns is the absence from the streets and stores of ladies whose apparel and demeanor would indicate them as of well-to-do families. Their absence arises from the fact that it is generally regarded as a proceeding of doubtful respectability for a lady to go about the streets, unless accompanied by a duenna or by some male member of the family. These are not always available, and the processes of marketing and shopping are commonly carried on through servants or by means of messengers from the stores.

One also misses certain kinds of American stores, notably those connected with food supplies. The markets close at noon. All purchases of meats, vegetables, and fruits are supposed to be, and must be, made before that hour. I did not learn the resources for supplies in the case of the arrival of unexpected guests, whose presence would necessitate a more extensive provision than that made for the family. One could not send around the corner, or a few blocks down the street, and get a roast, or a chop, or a fowl, a fish, or a steak, at any time when it might be wanted. There was no convenient provision store, or green-grocer, from which one could obtain a bit of lettuce or a bunch of celery. There was no convenient fruit-store. Here and there, in some out-of-the-way corner, one might find a little shop where some kinds of fruit, and possibly a few vegetables, might be obtained; but the stock of such places was not particularly tempting. One missed also the American grocery-store, with its cleanly kept assortment of attractive foods. To market or to shop in these places one must go through a process of special education, to learn just where to go for the things wanted. No doubt Porto Rican ways are just as good as American ways, when one becomes accustomed to them; but at first one is struck by the seeming incongruity of finding hardware and saddlery in a dry-goods store; of buying potatoes and cigarettes in a place which gives all evidence of being devoted to the sale of *delicatessen*, and of buying bread and native rum over the same counter. The adjustment of lines of merchandise in Porto Rico savors, in many cases, of the back-country districts of Maine and North Carolina.

A good knowledge of the Spanish language is of

course a desirability in any Spanish or Spanish-American country. But it is not a necessity. There may be times when one has to sacrifice a bit of dignity in order to get what is wanted, but most of us have enough of that to be able to spare a little of it. I saw one chap, at a breakfast-table, flap his arms while he imitated the cackle of a hen and formed an ovoid with his thumbs and fingers. But he got the eggs he wanted. One gets along very well by remembering two words and carrying a small list of Spanish names for common articles. *Quiero* (ke-á-ro) means, "I want," and *cuanto* (koo-ahn-to) is an abbreviation for a sentence which means, briefly, "how much?" It is all very simple. Say "quiero," and the name of the thing wanted; then say "cuanto," and produce all the money you have, and permit the one with whom you are dealing to help himself to all he wants; then take your purchase and your departure, saying, "*muchas gracias*" (many thanks). This latter expression serves a double purpose. It gives the dealer an idea you are thanking him for what he has done for you; but it is in reality your expression of gratitude to a beneficent Providence that, out of your little store of wealth, that dealer has left you even a few centavos. But it is not necessary to learn "*muchas gracias*." Just say, "Thank you," and grin, exactly as one does when leaving the dentist whose kindly services have spared one's life, and no more.

My own command of Castilian was only a little less deficient when I came away than it was when I arrived out. Yet I spent three months there and travelled over the greater part of the island. I admit that it was a little awkward at times, but I always contrived in some way to get what I wanted, if it was obtainable, and to get where I wanted to, if the roads were passable. Some might recommend another verb, such as the interrogatory of the verb "*tener*," to have, in place of my, to me, quite satisfactory, "*quiero*." But "*tiene usted*" asks a question which may involve a further conversation. Thus, if one wants eggs with his breakfast, and says to the waiter, "*Tiene usted huevos*," the waiter may simply reply, "*Si, Señor*." Then the señor must be able to go on with "*Traigame dos huevos, al plato*," or something of the kind. My "*quiero dos huevos*" informs him at once that "I want two eggs." If he replies, "*Si, Señor*," I know that he will bring them without further conversation. If he says, "*No hay*," I know that the house is out of eggs, and that I must fish around in my vocabulary for something else to "*quiero*."

In travelling one most "wants" the things which are essential—food, a bed, and means of transportation. A brief list of nouns and names is easily committed to memory. Additions will be readily made to the list as one moves about. Such a list, supported by the useful *"quiero,"* and the almost equally useful " *cuanto,*" and such other words as came to me during my wanderings, took me through cities and towns, and over many miles of Porto Rican highways.

V

INTO THE COFFEE DISTRICT

The Town of Yauco—The Sunday Morning Market—Fruits and Vegetables—Jacky and the Natives—Guanica—Our First Landing Place—A Horse Trade—On the Road to Adjuntas—A Mountain Town—The Good Padre—The Kitchen-maid and her Cigar.

YAUCO and Guanica are two of the places which are said to have been captured by the American forces on the island of Porto Rico. Yauco is the principal place and is quite a little city. Guanica is a straggling village on the coast, some six miles to the southward of Yauco, for which place it serves as a port and as a summer-resort for the well-to-do citizens of its larger neighbor. Yauco is the present terminus of the Ponce and Yauco division of the Compania de los Ferrocarriles de Puerto Rico. The drainage of Yauco is admirable. The town stands on a hill-side which is about as steep as the roof of a house. The business portion of the town, and its better buildings, are upon the lower slopes, while cottages and cabins straggle away to the higher and steeper regions. The town has a considerable French population, though I am told that the majority are Corsican rather than French.

The place is the commercial centre for a considerable district of productive back country, and one of the outlets, through its port city of Guanica, for the coffee district. One of the interesting sights, for the visitor, is the plaza on Sunday morning. So far as my observation goes, the people of Porto Rico go to market on Sunday morning instead of going to church. Had I seen as many people in church that Sunday as I saw buying and selling on the plaza, I should have set Yauco down as a religious, if not a pious, place. As it was the church was deserted, while the plaza was packed with a throng of chattering traders which numbered some fifteen hundred people. The entire square was bordered with ox-carts and pannier-laden ponies belonging to people the most of whom had come to sell twenty-five cents' worth of fruit or vegetables, and to buy a few cents' worth of something they wanted. I confess to a personal disregard of the day to the extent of an interesting hour among the crowd, and the purchase of sundry fruits for the purpose of learning the prices. American money was then bringing a premium of seventy-five per cent. Ten cents, Porto Rican, was therefore, the equivalent of about six cents American. I bought a large, fine pineapple for ten cents, Porto

Rican. I paid twelve cents for a large muskmelon. I bought oranges at two for a cent, lemons at three for a cent, guavas at six for a cent, all Porto Rican money.

Most of the trading was done upon a small scale. The seller arranged his or her little stock of wares upon a mat on the ground, dividing it into little piles which sold for one or two centavos per pile according to the ruling prices of the article offered. Squashes were cut into sections of suitable sizes. The purchase of a whole squash would probably cause the purchaser to be suspected of lunacy. The variety offered gives some idea of agricultural possibilities, though nothing which is cultivated gives evidence of proper care or development. Things are evidently planted and left to a kindly nature for results. If the beneficent dame sees fit to put nothing on a tomato vine any larger than a robin's egg, and nothing on an egg-plant any larger than one's fist, the native accepts the situation and appears to be satisfied. The collection offered included a large variety of native fruits, mangoes, cocoa-nuts, guavas, quenapas, lemons, oranges, pineapples, pomegranates, and others whose names are unfamiliar to us. In garden vegetables, there were beans, green peas, corn, peppers, egg-plant, melons, yams, and squashes. I saw none of the root-plants here, such as beets, turnips, and

Market-Place at Ponce.

carrots, though I saw some of them in the market at Ponce. Garlic was there in quantity. But that speaks for itself.

The Sunday morning market service begins at an early hour, and lasts until about noon, when all that has not been sold, and all that has been purchased and not eaten on the spot, is packed on the carts or in the panniers, and the congregation starts in every direction on its homeward way. It has transacted its little business, and has heard the news and the gossip which will form the basis for its conversation during the week. It seems a petty life, but it is the life of thousands. I saw it in the town of Adjuntas as I saw it here, and in the larger Ponce as I saw it in these country towns. Though the plaza is the common work-day market-place for such towns as have no regular market building, Sunday is the great market day.

During one of the days spent in Yauco, my attention was attracted by repeated shouts in the street. Upon going to investigate the occasion of the disturbance, I found that it was caused by a semi-intoxicated jacky from one of the monitors lying in Guanica Bay. Jacky was celebrating a day of shore-leave by experimenting with the sailing qualities of a Porto Rican pony. He was cruising up and down the principal street at a six-knot gait, and shouting at the top of his voice, "Viva Porto Rico." This was answered by the vigorous yells of some two hundred natives who were assembled, "Viva los Americanos," "Viva Puerto Rico Americano." There was no question of their sincerity. No man would yell as they did without meaning it. Jacky would howl his "Viva Porto Rico," and the crowd would come back at him with its vociferous response. All hands were having a good time. A little squad of the provost guard marched up to see what was going on. It grinned and marched back again.

The road from Yauco to Guanica takes one immediately past the scene of the first "battle" on Porto Rican soil. The Spanish army, consisting of a small company of soldiers, occupied the spacious yard which surrounds the large house and extensive outbuildings of M. Mariani, a French sugar-planter of great wealth and of long residence on the island. A high brick wall along the southern side of the yard formed the Spanish defence, from which point of vantage they exchanged a few leaden compliments with the American soldiery of General Henry's command which was posted on the hill beyond. After a few hours of no very energetic warfare, during which a small casualty list was made upon both sides, the Spaniards withdrew to make room for a deputation of the prominent citizens of Yauco, who extended a warm hand of welcome to the invaders, and declared it their pleasure to become a part of the American people. This episode ended the war in the immediate vicinity, and the so-called " battle " wound up with a reception.

Guanica is a pretty little harbor, with a narrow entrance, flanked by high hills, which descend sharply to the water's edge. It presents possibilities as a seaside resort. Its surroundings are charming. A pleasant and refreshing breeze blows from off the water. Pleasant drives could easily be laid out, which would take one either among the mountains or along the coast. There is still-water bathing inside the headlands and surf-bathing beyond them. There is said to be duck-shooting on a near-by lake, and there is dove-shooting in the forest for those who like pot-hunting. Just now Guanica is rather out of the world, but the construction of a Porto Rico belt-line railroad, and the visits of the American tourist, will be likely to make a considerable difference in the life of what is now a sleepy but a beautiful little spot.

The "Military Notes of Puerto Rico," a small pamphlet issued by the government for the benefit of commanding officers in that island, gives Adjuntas as follows: " Adjuntas, a town of 2,320 inhabitants, with a jurisdiction numbering 18,820; situated fifteen and a half miles from Ponce. It has a post-office and a telegraph station." Adjuntas is another of the Porto

Rican towns which we "captured." It was taken by General Roy Stone, who rode into it, accompanied by a score or so of soldiers, as he made his way across the island to Arecibo for the purpose of investigating the condition of the highways in that portion of the island. At army head-quarters, General Stone's invasion of the region was regarded as somewhat premature. That route was to have been traversed by a triumphant army under the command of General Guy V. Henry. As matters stood, there was no glory to be got out of it, but General Stone's preliminary excursion robbed it of what little of *éclat* might possibly have attached to it.

I began my personal campaign against the conquered city of Adjuntas by the purchase of a horse for 100 pesos, or about $50 in American money. The size of the beast left me in doubt as to the easiest way to carry him with me, whether in my grip-sack or in my pocket. But I decided that, as I had bought him for the purpose of riding him, I would make use of his four legs to aid my own two. His former owner drove him into the proper position between my legs, and I sat down on him. But there was as far as he would go. I applied the spur, and he started upward, but not onward. As my immediate destination was Adjuntas and not the spacious firmament, I stood up and cancelled the trade. I decided to hire instead of buy. I referred to my vocabulary, and said: "*Quiero un coche para Adjuntas, mañana,*" which was as near as I could come to saying that I wanted a "carriage for Adjuntas, to-morrow." I said it to all the proprietors of carriages who would listen to me, and their name was legion. I supplemented it with a very business-like "*cuanto?*" After an hour or so of saying "*si*," and "*bueno*," to something like a thousand questions and statements of which I did not understand one single word, I succeeded in contracting for "*un coche, un cochero, y dos caballos,*" or, a carriage, a driver, and two horses, for about ten per cent. less than their assessed valuation. The party of the second part assured me that it would be necessary to send on two relays for so great a journey—fifteen and a half miles.

I was breakfasting on hardtack and "slum" with my good friends of C Battery of the Seventh Artillery, when my "*coche y cochero*" appeared on the following morning. The first six or seven miles of the journey to Adjuntas are over a fairly level and well-made macadamized road, past acres of banana-groves and through a country of great beauty and attractiveness. As the road winds and twists around the hill-sides farther back from the shore, the valleys open up long vistas to the southward, with the ocean for a background. Much of it, except for the distant water, brought strongly to mind some of the wilder and more precipitous portions of the North Carolina mountains in its general topography. There is but little level ground. The area is almost wholly destitute of those "bottom lands," which are usually found among the hill countries. Cottages by the wayside were literally perched there. The front sill lay immediately upon the edge of the roadway, while the rear of the house rested upon supports of eight or ten feet in height, so steep was the slope in many cases.

Here and there one finds a more pretentious villa on the crest of a little knoll, with a more or less fantastic arched gateway bearing the name of the place, a common practice in Spanish countries. Contrasted with these houses of better type, one sees the rude cabin with its rough framework covered with the large sheets of the fibrous bark, which finds a general use in lands where is found growing the species of palm from which the material is obtained. Many of these structures are exceedingly picturesque, but their principal advantage would seem to lie in the fact that one can throw anything which is not wanted out of the back window, and see it roll away down the hill for any number of feet. It disposes of all manner of refuse and *débris* without littering up the back-yard.

It is a somewhat tedious ride to climb the long hill on the Adjuntas road, and the enjoyment of the ride is modified by the fact that, out of consideration for the wretched little beasts used on the island as carriage-horses, the merciful man is compelled to walk the greater part of the way. With such a road as might be easily constructed the trip would be wholly delightful. Brilliant flowers, giant yuccas, palms, and brakes which assume almost tree-like proportions, border the highways and cover the hillsides. Banana-groves, the rich dark green of the mango-trees, and all the foliage and undergrowth of the tropics; the winding road opening an unbroken series of exquisite landscape pictures; and the dashing mountain-streams plunging and tumbling over rocky beds and falls, give the nature-lover a continuous feast along this beautiful bit of a beautiful country. The crest of the hill is reached about two miles out of Adjuntas, and a sharp descent brings the traveller into the valley to follow the course of a merry little stream, past quaint little homes which lie in the suburbs of the town; and, at last, to the door of a quaint little hotel where one gets a fair bed, and a very good meal, and a cordial welcome.

The district of which the town of Adjuntas is the principal centre, includes a large slice of the best coffee-growing territory of the island. There the coffee industry assumes very considerable proportions, and one sees the plant growing upon all sides. An excellent article is produced, and good prices are usually obtained for it. The greater portion of the crop finds its market on the European continent. A Porto Rican coffee plantation does not present any very marked difference in appearance from the rest of the country. The bush, or shrub, growing to some eight or ten feet in height, is set out on no apparent system, and grows mixed up with bananas and forest timber. Until one knows what it is, one might easily pass a whole plantation and believe that he had seen nothing but a somewhat scattered forest with its usual undergrowth of scrub and thicket. Locally, the coffee is served in small cups, and is very black and very strong. But it is also excellent.

The town proper occupies a beautiful location in a narrow valley, whose borders rise sharply and steeply to the summits of the surrounding hills. A little stream, which the people of the place dignify with the title of El Rio (the river), runs through the town, and makes itself very useful for laundry purpose *à la* Porto Rico. In the heart of the village an open space is turned into a public park, with crosswalks, shrubbery, and brilliant flowers. It is not over-neatly kept, and there is no particular evidence of skilful gardening; but the place is quite attractive, and constitutes a pleasant relief to some of its rather dingy surroundings. Here and there a private residence shows a rank garden-growth of bright-hued flowers. But, on the whole, the long and straggling town is not particularly attractive. Most of its houses are mere cabins, and few of even the better class are at all home-like, from the American standpoint. The Spanish people and their kindred would seem to have but two ideas regarding a residence. There appears to be no mean between the *casa*, with its *patio*, abutting immediately upon the sidewalk and wall to wall with others very much like it, and the country-seat a good distance from any neighbors. Naturally, the poorer classes can have neither; but in a country where land is sufficiently abundant, there is no visible reason for setting every little cabin immediately upon the edge of the roadway, and within two or three feet of the buildings on either side of it.

The city hall is an unpretentious structure, one story in height, and painted, like many Porto Rican buildings of all classes, a pale blue, with white trimmings. In it are the offices of the alcalde, a functionary who seems to be something more than a mayor and something less than a governor. There are also the offices of the different legal and official dignitaries of the district. From the numerical relation of the police force to the population, one might infer that Adjuntas was a sort of Porto Rican "Bitter Creek," where everybody was bad, and the higher up one went, the more and more wicked he found the people. In the United States, a village which needed a policeman to every hundred of its inhabitants, would be shunned by all, and would soon be deserted by all who did not stay behind for the express purpose of killing each other. Such a town in the United States would have a constable or two, or a marshal with a deputy.

Adjuntas claims a population of 2,300, and has a chief of police with a force of twenty men under him. They are in ample evidence in the principal streets, dressed in suits of linen with narrow blue-and-white stripe, and wearing a belt and a sword. They are a rather light-weight lot, and a fair specimen of the Bowery tough would probably have but little trouble in doing up a half-dozen or so of them in the course of an evening, without breaking his gait.

The spiritual needs of the community are cared for by a most excellent man. It is a pleasure to render even so slight a tribute to the good Padre Antonio Millon, the parish priest of Adjuntas. Although a Spanish sympathizer, this gentleman sunk all else, and remembered only those words, spoken so many centuries ago, "If thine enemy hunger, feed him; if he thirst, give him drink." When the great government of the United States was sending its soldiers into the field without adequate provision for them in case of sickness, Padre Antonio Millon gave his time, his care, and his thought to nursing, feeding, and caring for the sick soldiers of the United States army.

Among those to whom this good man ministered was a soldier of the Nineteenth Infantry. For a week the soldier lay at the point of death, faithfully nursed and tended by the good priest. But the case was hopeless. During his illness, the battalion to which the soldier was attached had moved forward to Utuado. Authority was obtained, by the army telegraph line, from the commanding officer, for the burial of the dead man in Adjuntas. All suitable arrangements were made by the padre, and the soldier was laid to rest under the shadow of the Porto Rican hills. I reached Adjuntas on the day of the burial, and learned of the incident soon after my arrival.

Late in the afternoon I had the pleasure of meeting Padre Millon. He came to my hotel to ask me to attend, as a representative of the country to which the dead soldier had belonged, a mass service at the little church in the village. The soldier had not been of the Catholic faith, but the padre put away all questions of nation and creed, and saw only a soul. Feeling that all possible recognition of the good priest's kindly service and broad charity was none too much for Americans to show, I spoke to Captain Jackson, the commanding officer of a company of the Sixth Massachusetts, then doing provost guard duty in Adjuntas, and to Captain Brown of the First Illinois, who arrived the same day with a little group of the Provisional Engineer Corps, on their way from Utuado to Ponce.

Both of these gentlemen fully appreciated the situation, and at seven o'clock on the following morning every man of their respective commands not detailed for routine duty, was in the lines which were drawn up inside the church. Some sixty soldiers were thus present, with such observance of military form as was possible under the circumstances. At the close of the service the provost guard returned to its quarters, the engineers marched away on their long tramp to Ponce, and the priest took up his daily round of parish duties. All honor to the good padre with the broad badge of the Spanish Red Cross Society on the shoulder of his priestly cassock.

Adjuntas has stores. It has many of them. From all appearances the majority of them either carry a stock of liquor as an adjunct to a stock of miscellaneous merchandise, or a stock of miscellaneous merchandise as an adjunct to a bar-room. I was told that there were no restrictions there upon the sale of liquor, and I could see no evidence of any. Yet I saw no intoxication. Almost every one drinks wine and native rum, and occasionally there is a disturbance in which the omnipresent machete plays its little part. The women smoke both cigarettes and cigars. Occasionally one meets a woman, evidently of the poorer classes, sauntering along the street, puffing a full-grown cigar. Sitting in my room in Adjuntas I could look from my window into the rear yard of the hotel, and see a dark-skinned, though not black, woman, washing the dishes from the dinner-table. The dish-washing did not seem to be much of a treat, but she surely enjoyed the cigar from which she extracted such a volume of smoke. Her assistant, a smaller and lighter-skinned damsel, was also smoking. Ladies of higher social grade are a bit more shy about their public performances on the cigar.

The attractiveness of Adjuntas lies more in its surroundings than in its streets or its houses. The steep hills, wild and many folded, rise sharply on all sides, rich with color and verdure. A short walk from the hotel took one into the heart of it all, and away from " wars and rumors of wars "; from muddy camps and all their turmoil.

VI

A NIGHT IN THE SADDLE

Correspondents on the Firing-line—An Excited Chief of Police—Beyond the Outposts—A Search for Willing Prisoners—A Blind Trail—A Spaniard's Hospitality—Midnight Encounters—Friends or Foes—Unwilling Rough Riders—A Striking Picture—The Capture—" Too Near " Home.

THE Porto Rican campaign was decidedly lacking in opportunities for newspaper correspondents to ascertain the measure of their resources in the matter of personal heroism. During the days which followed the occupation of Ponce, a few trifling engagements took place in the immediate vicinity of the city. The "firing-line" was reached by a pleasant drive over an admirable road which traversed a region full of delight and interest to the nature-lover. These engagements were duly attended by a few correspondents, and there is no doubt that all maintained a due and proper degree of placidity and serenity under the ordeal of facing bullets which were flying principally in directions other than that of their particular position. One or two did hear the whistle of Mauser bullets.

One venturesome spirit bought a horse and rode out gallantly with the purpose of entering San Juan at a time when the enterprise presented a somewhat doubtful outcome. He returned confessing, very honestly, that he got "rattled" when within a few miles of the city. He would really have been far more safe in entering it than in riding back over the mountains. Aside from the risk of danger to life and limb which lay in carriage journeys over various Porto Rican highways, my own opportunities for courting death or capture at the hands of the enemy were limited to a nocturnal expedition beyond our outposts, for the purpose of assisting in bringing in some Spanish prisoners who were anxious to be captured. They stood in greater fear of their compatriots than of their nominal enemies.

At the time of the signing of the Protocol, General Garrettson's brigade was on its way across the island to Arecibo. A battalion of the Nineteenth Regulars occupied Utuado and the Sixth Massachusetts and Sixth Illinois were in camp at Adjuntas, some ten miles farther south. I had left Ponce the day before with the intention of going across the country to Arecibo, where I purposed taking the train for San Juan. My route took me through the territory occupied by this brigade, which formed the expedition commanded by General Guy V. Henry. The news of the signing of the Protocol reached me at Adjuntas, and introduced an element of uncertainty regarding the status of Americans within the Spanish lines, and the right of even American civilians to cross the frontier. I decided to remain at Adjuntas until I could obtain fuller information, deeming it wise to risk no interference with the work I was doing, for no greater prospective equivalent than the possibility of a sensational story of a few days of detention in a Spanish prison.

Just before noon of my second day in Adjuntas, my friend Captain Johnston, of the Sixteenth United States Infantry, then serving as quartermaster on the staff of General Henry, came to my room in the little hotel where I was staying, to invite me to accompany him on an excursion into the country toward Lares, a region that was still in possession of the Spanish forces. It had been reported to the local chief of police that some eighteen or twenty men, *voluntários* who had evaded service, and deserters from the Spanish army, were at a plantation three or four miles beyond the city. They wished to come in but feared the possible violence of the people, and therefore desired an armed escort to protect them. The chief was greatly excited. He referred the matter to Captain Johnston, who decided to give it his personal attention. The details were rather

Cathedral and Plaza at Arecibo.

vague, and the promise of excitement was rather limited.

But the expedition offered at least a pleasant ride into the country, and the possibility of a novel experience. I was quite ready to accept the invitation. We ordered an early lunch, and were in the saddle soon after noon. It was not a regular military affair. Our party consisted of the captain and myself, an orderly, an interpreter, the chief of police, and ten of his men. The captain was mounted on a big chestnut horse, and the orderly rode a remarkably long-legged army mule. The rest of us looked as imposing as we could on the little native horses, whose height seldom exceeds twelve to thirteen hands. The police were armed with the old-fashioned Remington rifle, with swords, and with pistols if they possessed them. The orderly carried the Krag-Jorgensen rifle of our regular army. The captain and I carried 38-calibre Colts of the latest army pattern, and the interpreter carried an umbrella.

A ride of a mile or two beyond the city, over a fairly good road which wound through coffee plantations and banana groves, brought us to the border of a little stream. Upon its bank stood an American soldier. Near him there floated, from the top of a rude pole, a bit of white cloth. His position marked the boundary of the American occupation, and the bit of white linen at the end of the pole was the flag of truce, which indicated, for a time at least, peace between the warring nations. On the other side of the stream we were on Spanish soil. We had started on a basis of a short ride of three or four miles, but the farther we rode the less our little chief of police seemed to know about his destination. "*La casa*" —*the* house, became "*Una casa*"—*a* house. The sun was broiling hot, and the road became more and more rough and uneven the farther we went.

At four miles out "*a* house" was still somewhere beyond. Five miles brought us no certainty. We interviewed householders and such travellers as we met. The willing prisoners of the conquering nation might be at any one of a half dozen places, but all were "*mas adelante*"—farther on. At about the sixth mile, Johnston and I consulted. We cross-examined the little chief. He knew nothing. He only felt sure that the object of our search was "farther on." We decided to push forward. There was no way of telling what might happen. The message to the police might be wholly correct except for an error in point of distance. It might be wholly false. It might even be a trap with mischief in it. We rode on. Our police escort was beginning to lag a little. Two or three times we had to wait for them, and once or twice Johnston used the imperative in telling the chief to order his men to "close up." The idea grew upon us that they did not quite like the job. They were not stalwart six-footers—these police. That sort does not grow there. I doubt if any one of them weighed a hundred and twenty pounds, and a diet of plantains, beans, and rice does not make men of brawn and muscle.

At four o'clock we had covered a little more than eight miles. At that point we came to a large and most comfortable-looking mansion which proved to be the residence of one Señor Antonio Mayol, a prosperous coffee planter. We dismounted to rest in the shade of his large coffee-house, and were soon surrounded by a numerous company of the people of the plantation. For a few moments we were in some doubt of their attitude toward us. The little chief whispered "Español." That was true. Señor Mayol was of Spanish birth, and was presumably loyal to his country. But whatever the Spanish official may be as a governor of colonies, the Spanish private citizen has but one fault as a host. He overdoes things in the matter of hospitality. His guest must eat more than he ought, drink more than he wants, and accept courtesies until they become little short of oppressive. Of this type was our host, who soon bustled his way through the group of spectators. His cordial welcome was hardly over before Juan and José and Pedro were sent scurrying away to return in an incredibly short time with refreshments for our party.

Señor Mayol assumed that we had come to stay with him and gave orders for the unsaddling of our horses. After a little time and difficulty we were able to make him understand our errand, and from him we received the first information we had been able to obtain, which was even approximately accurate. Our vague party of prisoners seemed likely to take on a tangible form at a farm-house five miles beyond, and on the other side of the mountain. The broad veranda of Señor Mayol's house looked very attractive, and the hot mountain-side looked very hot and very steep. It was suggested that as the police had got us into the scrape, the police should get us out. Captain Johnston, the interpreter, the orderly, and the writer, would rest at Señor Mayol's. The police should proceed and bring the prisoners to us, instead of taking us to the prisoners. The chief demurred, but Johnston is tall and has square shoulders and a determined expression. The police moved on, with positive instructions to be back before seven o'clock at the latest.

We spent the intervening hours most pleasantly as Señor Mayol's guests. He set forth an over-abundant dinner, showed us his estate, his gardens, and his mills. Neither war nor politics came into our conversation, and those few hours have in them nothing save kindly thoughts and pleasant memories. Darkness came as we smoked an after-dinner cigar on the cool veranda, but the police did not come. Seven, and the half past, came without bringing them, and we began to speculate concerning their whereabouts and their experience. Had they deserted us? Were they in trouble? As it stood, we could not get back to Adjuntas before midnight at the best, and we wanted to get back.

Shortly before eight o'clock the son of our host, a fine young fellow of twenty or so, volunteered to ride up the road for any news he might be able to pick up. He had been gone about twenty minutes when the sound of rapid hoof-beats announced that somebody was coming up in a hurry. It proved to be young Mayol, trembling with excitement. We learned that he had been "held up" and threatened with a beating at a place about a mile and a half from his home. He was the son of a Spaniard and his assailants were Porto Ricans who hated him because of his race. He had got away and had sent his horse homeward at top speed. The incident determined our movements. We sent a "hurry call" to the stable for our horses, resumed the weapons that we had laid aside, and said "*Adios*" to our kindly host. Our purpose was to find the assailants of young Mayol if we could do so, and then to hunt up our missing police. Three or four of the farm people joined us with their machetes tucked under their arms, ready for use if the occasion arose. Young Mayol accompanied us to identify the chaps if we came across them. Of course they were not to be found. Ten or a dozen horsemen give sufficient notice of their approach to enable any who wish to do so, to avoid a meeting by escaping into the darkness.

We came to a house where quite a group of men had assembled, and stopped to question them. In the dim light I could see Johnston's hand swing around to his hip, just as mine did. I saw the barrel of the orderly's Krag-Jorgensen drop into the hollow of his left arm, and I could imagine just where his right hand was. But the interview was peaceable enough, and we learned nothing, save that the men we wanted had been there and had gone away, and that nothing had been seen of our police since their passing on their way out. We also learned that there was another route, which it then seemed probable that the police might have taken for their return. We decided to investigate the police question along the line of this other route. We reduced our party to the original group, except that we took one of Señor Mayol's people as a pilot over the hills.

Then followed what seemed an endless ride through the darkness. The main road had been too rough for comfortable riding through the gloom. Our new way was not even a road. It was but one of the many bridle-paths over the mountains which the natives use for getting about from plantation to plantation. I can give no description of it, except that at times we were in inky blackness under the dense foliage, obliged to call to each other in order to keep together, while at other times we were in open fields on the hill-tops with the bright stars to give us light, and the cool moisture-laden night air to give us rheumatism and influenza. I know that we forded rocky torrents on the mountain-side, that we rode up places that seemed like walls, and that we rode down places that seemed like precipices. Our horses stumbled and fell. My guiding star throughout the whole was that orderly sergeant on the tall mule. In the narrow way we could only ride in single file, and the mental photograph of that figure riding before me, vaguely outlined in the starlight of that night in August, will never be wholly obliterated.

Hour after hour we rode up, down, and around those hills. Ten o'clock and eleven o'clock passed, and there was no sign of our lost police. Once, as we turned a sharp corner, we came suddenly upon two white-garbed horsemen. Who they were, or how many might be behind them, we could not see. Again I saw that Krag-Jorgensen drop across the sergeant's arm. Upon comparing notes with Johnston afterward, I learned that his six-shooter was in his hand. I know that mine was ready. But the two white-clad apparitions proved to be the whole of the unknown force, and they appeared to be more frightened than we were, for they gave an indistinct answer to our challenge, and pushed their horses out of the path and into a brushy field to avoid us. We set them down, with probable correctness, as a couple of runaway *voluntários* making their way to their homes somewhere in the vicinity, and not at all anxious to meet anything in uniform, either Spanish or American.

Just before midnight, after losing our way two or three times and being forced to retrace our steps to find our proper path, we came upon a large and rambling set of farm-buildings, fronted by a fenced enclosure, with a high gateway. By the dim light of a suspended candle-lantern we could see the moving forms of a score of men and a long row of picketed horses. They might be our missing police. They might be a Spanish outpost. I think that if it had been the whole of the Spanish army Johnston would have challenged it just the same. We rode up to the gate with the Krag-Jorgensen in the hollow of the sergeant's arm, and a couple of long-barrelled Colt's revolvers ready for instant use. Again our preparation was needless. We had only come upon a country pack-train preparing for an early morning start to the distant city. We rode into the yard, and all dismounted except the sergeant on the tall mule. He kept his perch like a sentinel on a high tower. While we were questioning the people regarding the things we wished to know, the sergeant called the captain's attention and announced the approach of a squad of horsemen. I shoved my bridle into the hand of the nearest native and ranged up alongside the captain, facing the gate. I saw something white in his hand. His revolver was an ivory-handled weapon, a trophy of his skill as a pistol shot. Behind us loomed the sergeant on the tall mule, equally ready with the pair in front of him to shoot if necessary. Again the pistols went back to their holsters. The new arrivals were our missing policemen with their prisoners.

It was a weird picture that was shown there in that tropic midnight. The little squad of policemen on their jaded horses, the group of natives in their scant but picturesque raiment, towering over all the sergeant on the tall mule, the whole thrown into shadowy relief by the starlight, with bits of high light showing sharply in the rays of the lantern. All was black and white in bustling movement around a centre in which stood the captain and his interpreter listening to the story told by the chief of police. Briefly he had at last found his men and was bringing them in. There they were—six of them. One had a pass from an American army officer that would have taken him anywhere, unquestioned, within the American lines. For the other five, it is seldom that one sees men who are quite as delighted at becoming prisoners of war as was that quintette. They were unarmed, but in the house from which one of them was taken, the police had found two shot-guns which would seriously imperil the life of anyone who might attempt to use them, and an old-fashioned revolver of French make, using the pin-fire cartridge. The revolver disappeared in the crowd in the darkness. I think that Johnston had an idea where it was. I had something more than an idea. I was wearing one of those shooting-coats made of light duck and fitted with very large pockets. I found the pistol in one of those pockets the next morning. It must have fallen in somehow as it passed from hand to hand.

That part of our work was done. We had found our police and received our prisoners. We sent them on their way to the city, appointing a rendezvous at a certain spot *en route*, for seven o'clock in the morning. Then we swung our tired legs over the backs of our tired horses, to ride for another two hours to a point where we could catch an hour or two of sleep and join the police at the appointed time and place. I shall remember that two hours' ride as long as I live. After we had ridden until it seemed as if it must be very near the morning, I called to the interpreter to ask how much farther we had to go. His English was not of the best and he evidently confounded the meaning of the words "too" and "very," for he replied that the place was "too near." I heard a grunt from the sergeant and something about the place as not being "too near" by some kind of a sight. The qualifying adjective was lost by an opportune stumble on the part of the tall mule. Risking the character of the missing adjective I sung out a cordial endorsement of the sergeant's reply. At last the barking of the dogs in the valley far below us, and a dim gray spot which could be nothing other than a white building, gave us the welcome sign that our journey was over. It had consumed more than six hours since our second start. Our tired brutes picked their way down the rough path and brought us to the ample court-yard of a large coffee estate. I have a vague idea of lights, greetings, a cup of native coffee, a long passageway leading to a bedroom, and then—"Sleep, sore labor's bath."

The whole experience was one of potential, rather than actual adventure, but, as I have said, the Porto Rican campaign was not rich in opportunities for real adventures, particularly for newspaper correspondents.

VII

TYPICAL TOWNS AND VILLAGES

"Shucks and Shacks"—Picturesque San German—"Hotel the Struggle"—A Restless Night—A Native Description of the Engagement at Hormigueros—Two Humble Heroes—A Notable Shrine—Beautiful Mayaguez—A Miniature Street-car Line—Public Buildings —The Casino

AMONG the Porto Rican towns from which we shall probably be looking for election returns within a few years, are Sabana Grande, San German, and Hormigueros. All are in the southwestern part of the island. San German is the largest of the three, and lies midway between the other two, along the road from Ponce to Mayaguez. Yauco lies to the eastward of them, about ten miles from Sabana Grande.

If one turns the "b" in Sabana into Castilian, as it is in Habana, he at once gets the clew to the meaning of the name; and it readily resolves itself into "the great," or "large savannah," and "Sabana Grande" describes itself as a broad, level, and fertile plain. It is true that the place is not altogether as level as a barn floor, but beyond the low range of hills to the westward of Yauco, the traveller enters a broad and extensive valley, which occupies a large portion of southwestern Porto Rico. It is a land of corn and sugar-cane. The land is evidently of exceeding fertility, and in spite of years of cultivation without fertilizers it still yields abundant harvests, and might readily be made even more prolific. The town itself is not much to boast of. There is the usual *iglesia*, or church, fronting the usual open square. There is a suitable proportion of the very dirty-looking little stores which are common to such villages. There is the same general air of decay which characterizes the average Porto Rican village. But Sabana Grande seems to possess an unusual number of buildings of the genus "shack." It appears to be composed mainly of long rows of rough and badly built shanties, which give the greater portion of the town the appearance of being utterly poverty stricken. Yet the people of the place do not look any more dirty, ragged, or hungry than a great many of their compatriots in other places.

Before many of the houses, immediately beside the roadway, mats were spread upon which corn, shelled from the cob, was drying in the sun. The whole place seemed reeking with corn. Bushels of it were thus drying in the bright sunshine. It hung in great bunches from the rafters inside the little dwellings, and lay in piles upon the porches. In the fields it stood, some of young growth and some of ripened ears ready for gathering. Apparently, one might have boiled green corn upon his table, if he so wished, every day of the year in Porto Rico. It would mean but a little calculation of the time of planting. One of the leading citizens, at whose house I stopped in passing, gave me oranges and pomegranates picked from the trees as we walked through his garden. He showed me his young coffee-shrubs, growing in the shade of the bananas. It appears that it will not do to expose the coffee-plant to the rays of the sun. It is, therefore, planted and grown under the shade of the banana or some tree whose growth outstrips the coffee in rapidity, and under whose leaves the more sensitive shrub finds the shelter which it needs.

San German is the next town on the route. It appears to be bisected by Luna Street, with the larger and more important portion of the place on the north side. It is an old town, claiming a foundation by Captain Miguel Toro, in 1511. The appearance of some portions of it would indicate an establishment of even more ancient date. A photographer who possessed an acute sense of the artistic could spend a week or two there very profitably, though perhaps not very comfortably. The cathedral, with its long flight of steps, almost as wide as the front of the edifice, would make a good subject, and some of the picturesque people and children could be posed on those stairs and some delightful studies be obtained. I noticed an old ruin, perhaps a church of an earlier date. With proper lights and shadows, it would yield some capital bits for the camera. So, too, with the town itself. Its narrow streets should yield an abundant harvest for the man with a good tripod instrument. But it is not a place for snap-shots. Few places are, if one wants pictures. The man who only wants a photograph can get it anywhere. In San German there are old iron fences of considerable height and elaboration of design, with massive stone pillars, enclosing tangled growths of tropical plants. There are plant-covered balconies on houses of the better class, and artistic dilapidation and decay among the houses of the older portions of the place.

Of all the dingy and unattractive hotels which I experienced on the island, the San German affair was the worst. But there was a picture in the flight of stone steps which led into it and opened at their upper end upon a sort of arched semi-inclosure, through which, from the stairs, the near-by hills stood in beautiful relief. The hotel was of the kind which one remembers, though not for its delights. From the corner of the building hung the signboard.

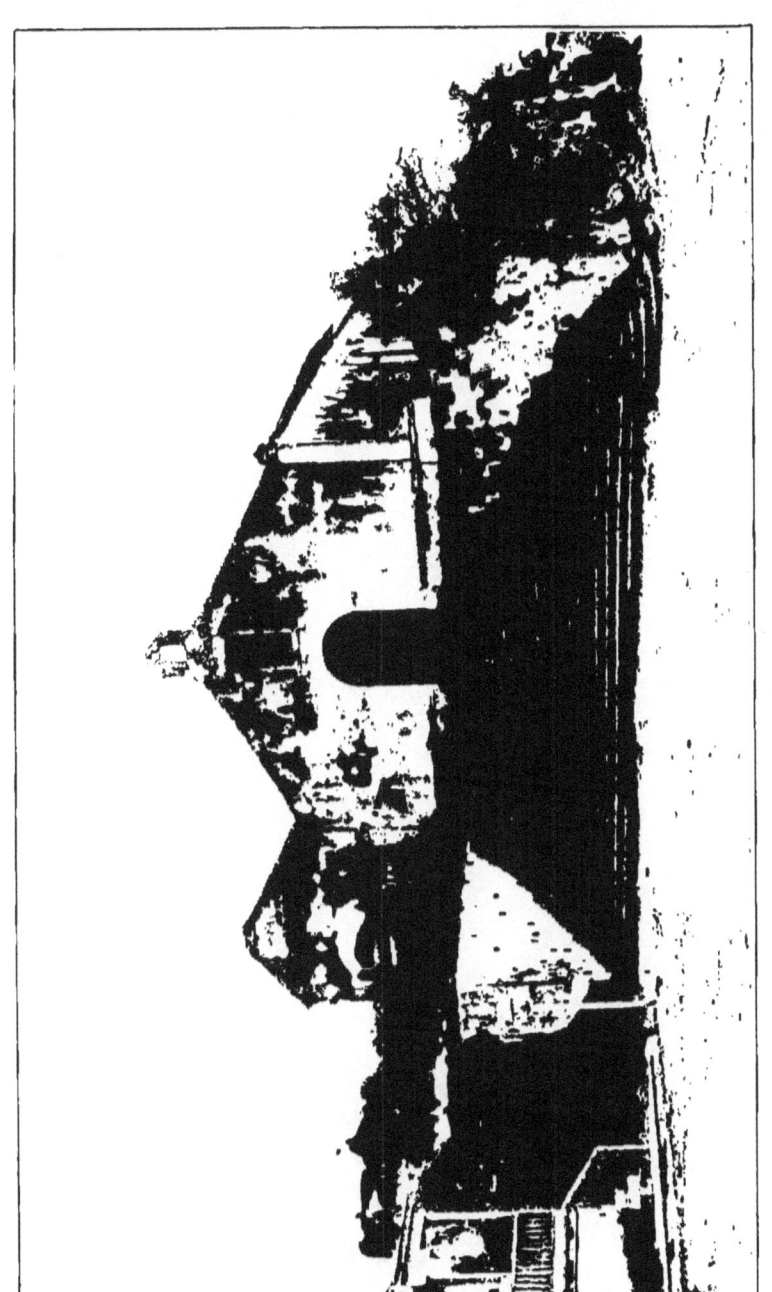

Dominican Monastery, in San German, Built about 1511.

"Fonda la Lucha." "Hotel the Struggle," would be a literal translation of the name of this hostelry. "Lucha" also means "strife." The special application of the name to the hotel is left to the ideas of the traveller. Possibly the proprietor struggles to make a living out of the place. Possibly the meaning touches the guest more closely than it does the host. He was a clever man, mine host, pleasant and obliging, but in his hotel I strove with ants on the dining-table, and struggled with fleas in my bedroom. I should hardly go as far as did Richard III., and decline to "pass another such a night, though 'twere to win a world of happy days," but I am not hungry to duplicate it.

I had every reason to believe that I was the only American in the city that night. I had no idea of the nationality or of the political opinions of my host. I presume that he was all right. But conversations which I overheard, and the appearance of one or two individuals who dropped in after nightfall, were not wholly reassuring, and I judged it wise to put my revolver under my pillow. What with the fleas and the feeling that I had best not sleep too soundly, the amount of sleep which I did not get that night would have well rested any man who was even more tired than I was. But it was cheap amusement. For my dinner, with a bottle of undrinkable wine, my lodging, and my breakfast, I paid a sum equal to about seventy-five cents in American money.

Hormigueros is not much of a town. Its chief interest to Americans just now is the fact that its vicinity gives the name to one of those little engagements which, in this rather opera-bouffe campaign, we denominate as "battles." There was a bit of sharp infantry firing, with a slight casualty list for both sides. But it was hardly even a skirmish fight. My driver illustrated the scene with great animation as I passed it on my way. His finger pointed out the line of march of the "Americanos." The index was suspended to indicate a certain spot. A vigorous and staccato "Pom-m-m," meant that the artillery had halted at that point and tried a shot or two. Then the word "Español," an animated rotary motion of the hands, and the pointing out of the hills behind the village, made sufficiently clear the manner in which the valiant Spaniards had tumbled over each other in their efforts to get away behind the summits which formed the picturesque background of the village of Hormigueros. It was not much of a fight, but it put the American flag in the place of a Spanish *bandera* over another Porto Rican town.

The Spaniards might have stopped the Americans twenty times within the next few miles. They might have decimated the American ranks by guerilla firing. They might have played the mischief with us, generally. But they appear to have been utterly "rattled." They would seem to have been terror-stricken by the appearance of an army which fired as it moved forward, and always moved forward. It was here that there occurred one of those little exhibitions of individual courage which are of greater frequency in the ranks of our regular army than is generally known to the public. Captain Hoyt's company of the Eleventh Regular Infantry was in advance. The Spanish troop were hunting cover and falling back with great agility. The side of the little hill which lay before the American lines was a cleared field. Its top was wooded and formed an admirable cover. The wood might be filled with Mausers. Captain Hoyt hesitated about sending his men across the clearing. Two men stepped from the ranks. One of them had been in the army for some years and had seen service on the plains. The other was of recent enlistment. With as much coolness as they would have shown in following a deer track, the two started up the slope at a trot, and plunged into the thicket. They soon reappeared with a cry to "come along." Then they disappeared, to repeat the process on the next hill. Who were they? I do not know. The army is full of such men. We hear very little about them. It is true that they might be well advertised as The Heroes of Hormigueros, because they did in a little way what Dewey and Hobson did on a larger scale. It is the way of the army and navy, that is all. All that is needed is the opportunity. Had it been necessary or desirable, the whole command would have gone as the two men did.

The little hillside village of Hormigueros possesses, in its church edifice, a venerated and widely known point of interest. Overlooking the village and the surrounding valley, stands the church of Our Lady of Monserrate. It is a holy spot, and has for many years been the gathering point for pilgrims who come, not only from other parts of the island, but, as well, from many of the adjacent islands of the Antilles. Its special distinction as a point for pilgrims arises from a glory borrowed from the celebrated Benedictine monastery in Spain, standing a few miles from the city of Barcelona. The Spanish monastery draws tens of thousands of pilgrims to its doors every year because of its possession of a statue said to have been carved by the apostle Luke, and brought to Barcelona, in the year 50, by the apostle Peter. The Hormigueros sanctuary would seem to stand as the local representative of the shrine whose name it bears. It is a picturesque structure, stand-

Plaza and City Hall in San German.

ing on the crest of a hill and reached by a long flight of steps. From the fact that my driver pointed it out to me as an army barracks, I infer that it was occupied by the Spanish troops before the arrival of the American army.

The pamphlet, issued by the government for the use of army officers, and entitled "Military Notes on Porto Rico," contains, among some facts, a considerable assortment of misinformation. Its maps and its statements are chiefly drawn from Spanish sources, and display the general inaccuracy of detail which marks the bulk of Spanish productions of that character. This pamphlet gives, under the head of "Mayaguez," the following: "A city of 11,615 inhabitants, with a jurisdiction numbering 28,026. The majority of the population is white. It is the third city in importance in the island, being situated in the west part facing what is generally known as 'Mona Channel.' It is a seaport of considerable commerce, and is one hundred and two miles from San Juan." A part of this is true, with limitations. Whatever else may be said for it, there is no question that Mayaguez is a beautifully situated city, and that it is well worth a visit. Its general architecture is, naturally, Spanish in its character. The greater number of its buildings are of stone or brick, and are one story in height. The wide portico extending across the front of the house, and raised from three to five feet above the sidewalk upon which it immediately borders, is the common fashion for the many well-built and well-painted residences which abound on the principal streets. Open doors and gates give views of pleasant interiors, and of court-yards filled with flowers and plants.

The streets are much wider than the usual thoroughfares of such places. Through some of them there runs a quaint little tram-road with a gauge of perhaps twenty-seven to thirty inches. The cars, which run at quite frequent intervals, are drawn by two of the little things commonly known as *caballos*, which translates into "horses." This is a reflection on the horse family. These cars cannot exceed twelve feet in length, and seem hardly that. Their width may be five and a half feet. They consist of a platform with a roof from which hang red and white striped curtains for protection against the sun and rain. There are two double seats, *dos-à-dos*, running across the car. The driver appears to divide his attention between his horses and any Americans who may ride with him.

The conductor is provided with a small pouch suspended by a strap over his shoulder. This is a receptacle for the fares collected, and the repository for a small book from which he tears a ticket for each

TYPICAL TOWNS AND VILLAGES 103

fare. He tears the ticket half in two as an indication that it has been used, and presents the mutilated scrap to the passenger as a receipt for money paid. This ticket, which is about two and one half inches square, has a central circular imprint, of about the diameter of a silver half-dollar, which reads, *Sociedad Anónima, Tranvia de Mayaguez.* Across the top it reads, *Consérvese durante el trayecto,* and across the bottom, *E inutilicese despues.* A random translation of this would turn it into "Hang on to this during your passage. It is good for nothing afterwards." I was informed that the street railway system was not remunerative, owing to the fact that affairs were left entirely to a superintendent whom nobody watched. It is now proposed to institute a reform and make a shot for some dividends. To that end, notices are now posted in the cars, on the under side of the roof, where one stands a fair chance of breaking his neck while reading them. They are to the effect that on and after the *28 de Agosto de 1898*, the fare will be increased from three cents to five, Porto Rico money.

The city proper is built on a rounded knoll, whose dome rises a hundred feet or so above the level of the beautiful bay, whose waters break gently upon its western base. The knoll is crowned by the central square. In the middle of this square stands a tall statue of Christopher Columbus, facing toward the sea to the westward. There is some conflict between different cities, of which Mayaguez is one, for the honor of being the point at which Christopher Columbus made his first landing on the island upon the occasion of his second voyage to the islands of the west. San Juan makes a claim which does not appear to be very well founded, and has erected a handsome monument to the memory of the distinguished navigator in one of its principal squares. Aguadilla, a pretty little city on the western coast, also presents a claim and has placed an imposing shaft, almost upon the very edge of the water, at the point which the citizens assert to have been the spot where the great man first set his foot on the island of Boriquén. Mayaguez also makes its claim for the distinction of being Christopher's first landing-place. In front of the monument is a somewhat imposing city hall, while behind it is a rather fine old cathedral, said to have been erected, I believe, in 1760. Westward, on the slope of the hill, stand the capacious infantry barracks, erected in 1848, and of sufficient size to accommodate nearly the whole of an American regiment. The city boasts of an elaborately designed theatre, a commodious market-house, a hospital, two asylums, a public library, electric lights, and an ice factory. From a Spanish-American stand-point, the city is quite modern and progressive. The social element finds a centre in the casinos, of which there are two. We should call them club-houses, although certain features are introduced not wholly common in American clubs.

I visited the one maintained and frequented by the Porto Rican element. The other, of Spanish tendencies and patronage, I did not see. My host for the day, a Porto Rican who was full of enthusiasm for the "American cause," informed me that he had never set foot in the Spanish club. He said that it was chiefly composed of men who hardly knew how to wear a collar, who did not know at all how to wear a coat, and who smelled of codfish. The Porto Rican casino occupies a palatial private residence rented for its purpose. At the head of the staircase is a large hall with chairs and a small grand piano. The spacious apartment occupying the entire front of the second story is designed for theatricals, and is equipped with a very complete little stage at one end. In the body and rear of the building are card-rooms, a library, a billiard-room, and a kitchen. Mayaguez evidently pays some attention to the business of enjoying itself.

The style of its residences and the demeanor of the people indicate a large measure of refinement, and a society of cultivated people. At the foot of the hill, alongside the water, one finds the wholesale business of the place. The custom-house is a creditable structure, and the warehouses are commodious and substantial. The harbor is not a particularly good one, though it probably could be made such. It is about three miles wide, and about a mile and a half from the shore to its entrance, across which there are dangerous shoals, requiring some caution on the part of sailing-masters. Vessels are unloaded by means of lighters, the usual way in Porto Rican harbors. The exports of the place are chiefly sugar and coffee, though a considerable quantity of fruit is also sent out. The coffee is mainly of two grades. The cheaper article finds its best market in Cuba, and the finer article, which ranks with the Javan product in quality and price, is almost entirely consumed by Europeans, who know good coffee when they get it. The American people do not seem to be very well acquainted with the excellences of Porto Rican coffee. The annual export of coffee from Mayaguez amounts to nearly 10,000 tons. The quantity of sugar exported is also very large, as the place is the shipping port for an extensive section of sugar-raising country.

At present the Mayaguez hotels are not to be highly recommended to American tourists, nor is the place itself readily accessible, except by means of direct steamship communication. Approaching from either Ponce or San Juan, one has twenty-five or thirty miles, by either route, which must be covered by private conveyance, and the roads for the greater part of the way are simply atrocious. After having gone in by means of a carriage, I dreaded to go out again, as one dreads a visit to the dentist. Some day this will doubtless be changed, and beautiful Mayaguez, with its lovely bay in front of it, and its charming hills behind it, will be equipped with attractive and comfortable hotels. The few miles of well-made roads in its immediate vicinity are heavily shaded avenues, with a picture in every rod of them. There should be good boating and bathing in the bay. Mayaguez might easily be made an exceedingly popular winter-resort, and if a visitor could be established in a comfortable hotel, there are many places doing a thriving business as summer-resorts which would hardly be in the running with Mayaguez.

VIII

FROM PONCE TO SAN JUAN

A Model Highway—A Bicycle Trip Worth Taking—Island Villages—The Baths of Coamo—Good Luck for our Army—A Mountain Drive—Passing the Outposts—Cayey and Guayama—Nature's Bounty—System of Road Repairs—Porto Rican Road-houses.

I SHOULD not know where to go in the United States to find a continuous hundred miles of highway to rival, in its general excellence, the road between Ponce and the capital of the island of Porto Rico. Were the road like the general run of the roads on the island, he who would essay the trip could safely be counted as either a brave or a reckless man. The line forms a part of a somewhat extensive system of military highways which were projected by the Spanish Government and paid for by the islanders. Few of them were completed more than a few miles from the cities from which they started. This connecting thoroughfare between the two chief cities was regarded, however, as of supreme importance, and was finished for its entire length, and a most creditable job was made of it.

The guide-book of military misinformation about Porto Rico gives various figures as the distance between Ponce and San Juan. It is placed at sixty-nine miles and at seventy miles. It is also given as "exactly 134 kilometres." The latter is doubtless correct, and it translates into near enough to a hundred miles to be set down as a "century run." Although the road crosses the mountains at an altitude of nearly, if not quite, 3,500 feet, there is very little of it which could not be traversed on a bicycle. From the height of land, coming southward, a rider could make a continuous coast of six or eight miles without touching a pedal or dismounting for rough spots. To the north of the backbone there is more of level road, with sharper declivities, though there is little or nothing which could rightly be regarded as a steep hill either upon the northern or the southern slope. After leaving Ponce, the road rises, by an almost imperceptible incline, along and through the foot-hills. The scenery is much like that of all the other parts of the island through which I travelled. Hills and mountains are always in sight upon one side or the other, if not upon both sides.

The road passes through the burned town of Coto Laurel, for the destruction of which sentences of rather dubious justice were pronounced against five men by the military commission which tried them for arson and pillage. It runs through the larger village of Juana Diaz, which is like all other towns of the island. There is the inevitable main street with its shambling structures at either end, improving by degrees toward the middle, where there is the inevitable church facing the inevitable plaza. Everywhere there is dirt and dilapidation. The streets are dirty and the stores are equally so. There is no air of neatness about either the towns or the people who inhabit them. Except that it is little more of a place, Coamo is like the others. The hotel duplicated previous experiences in other hotels. It was a dreary, barren, and cheerless place in which one got something to eat and a place in which to sleep.

The town of Coamo is one of the oldest on the island. It was founded in 1640. Its special distinction to-day is its thermal baths, which make it a place of resort not only for the Porto Ricans but for people from many of the surrounding islands. It is not easy to say just what will be done with these baths under the new order of things. It is wholly probable that they will become more widely known, and find a very great increase in their patronage. Of the genuine merit of the water as a cure for gout, rheumatism, and various other complaints, there can be no doubt. A judicious exploitation of the place may lead to its establishment as a fashionable Mecca for gouty and rheumatic

Cathedral and Plaza at Ponce.

American pilgrims. There is no reason why it should not find such a destiny. The situation of the town is charming, and it is easily reached by a fine drive of a little more than twenty miles.

Before the arrival of the Americans to disturb the social routine of the island people, the baths of Coamo offered no small attraction to its many guests in the facilities which it presented for winning or losing a few pesos, a year's income, or an entire fortune. Its reputation as a Porto Rican Monte Carlo rivalled its reputation as a Porto Rican Hot Springs. Gambling appears to have been one of the features of the resort, and many a visitor lost his money as well as his disease.

After leaving the town of Coamo, the road dips sharply down, by what is probably the steepest grade of the entire route from coast to coast, to a fine bridge which spans a modest little river. Then begins the gradual but continuous ascent to the top of the pass. This road was one of the routes by which it was proposed to reach the rear of San Juan for the assault upon that city.

To the unmilitary observer it would seem wholly futile to attempt the passage at all in the face of an enemy. Probably it never was the purpose of the American commander to do more than to make an active demonstration along the direct line of march while endeavoring to drive out the enemy by movements in flank and rear. But even that plan presented a desperate problem, and had General Miles made a careful personal inspection of the ground over which his troops were to fight, it is quite possible that the whole outline of the campaign would have been either changed or greatly modified. The confidence of the Spanish commander in the strength of his position was wholly warranted. The road presents point after point of the greatest exposure, from which but a mere handful of men could attack effectively only for the few brief moments during which they could withstand or outlive the fire of the enemy; flank movements could be made only by long and severe climbing of hill-sides standing at very steep angles. It is necessary to admit that the arrival of the notice of a cessation of hostilities may have meant our salvation from a sanguinary conflict, if not from a temporary defeat.

The winding of the road, as it bends in and out around the folds and ridges of the steep hill-sides, opens a series of ever-changing views in all directions. At one moment the traveller may be looking directly forward toward the top of the hill over which he climbs. A few minutes later his back may be toward his destination, while he finds himself facing directly down the valley out of which he is climbing, and looking upon the blue of the Caribbean Ocean in the distance as the background of a mountain picture. But I confess to a feeling of disappointment regarding the scenery. I had heard such tales of its marvellous beauty, its wild grandeur, and its overhanging cliffs, that I was led to expect more than I found. Beautiful it is, beyond denial, but I have seen scores of spots in our own White Mountains, the Alleghanies, and the Blue Ridge, which seem to me to be far finer than anything seen along the journey across Porto Rico.

On the occasion of my first trip across the island, the outposts of both armies were stationed at points near the crest of a hill, and within a short distance of each other. To go beyond our lines it was necessary to have a special pass from the military authorities. This was obtained at the head-quarters of the American forces, who were encamped just beyond Coamo. There, my companions and myself were received by General Ernst, the commanding officer, with that courtesy and kindliness which are so generally characteristic of our officers of the regular army. Immediately upon our introduction of ourselves, and the statement of our plans and wishes, General Ernst telegraphed to General Brooks, the military commander of the island, at San Juan, for instructions. After a surprisingly brief interval, a favorable answer came back, and the hoped-for pass, signed by General Ernst, was in our possession. The road was opened to us to go outside the American lines. Not far from the summit we came to the outpost of the Spanish lines, and were duly held up. Our pass allowed us to go through the American lines. Our further progress was a matter of courtesy on the part of the Spaniards. But they made less trouble for travellers, even for Americans, than did our own people. Yet the formalities of the American procedure, accompanied by the courtesy of the American general, were vastly preferable to the grim scowl with which the Spanish captain permitted us to go on our way. But he was wholly excusable. It was hardly to be expected that he would fall on our necks and bid us welcome. It was enough that he let us go.

From the top of the pass, northward, the character of the scenery changes quite noticeably. It is less wild and rugged, and there are evidences of a more general and more diversified cultivation of the soil. A short distance beyond the summit lies the town of Aibonito. The place itself belies its name as accurately as the surrounding hills and valleys support it. "Ah! Beautiful!" is the translation of the name; but it is not a suitable description of the town itself.

Yet it is a wholly characteristic Porto Rican town. Like the majority, it consists principally of a main street, a large church, with a plaza before it, a few central buildings of modest but dingy respectability, and a broad surrounding fringe of shacks and shanties. The principal difference between most of these larger Porto Rican towns lies in the fact that some are dirtier than others.

The next point on the way is Cayey. It is a larger Aibonito, with fifty years of added dinginess because of its earlier settlement. The directory of the island states that Cayey is a place of cool and pleasant temperature, producing coffee and all kinds of cereals. The difference in temperature between this region and the low coast-land is certainly very marked. One is hardly warranted in making positive statements regarding comparative temperatures unless supported by either a prolonged residence in the sections compared, or by the statistics of a weather bureau. But it was the common observation of those who crossed the island that the breezes which blew over the vicinity of Cayey brought a freshness and an invigoration which were not found elsewhere upon the island. There is, however, little doubt that the nights of the place share the general drawback of all the mountain area of Porto Rico. This lies in an excess of moisture, a cool dampness to which it is unwise and unsafe to expose one's self unduly.

At Cayey the main road is joined by the branch

which runs southward to Guayama. This road crosses some of the highest hills of the island, and presents some of the grandest views and most beautiful scenery of the territory. The verdure is perennial, and the time of year at which one might visit the place would make practically no difference in the richness of the foliage, which is the main feature of any expedition for pleasure made through the island. In all directions along this road from Cayey to Guayama, as elsewhere in all parts of Porto Rico, is a broad panorama of hills, their sides and tops robed with the yellowish green of pasture lands, the pale green of banana plantations, and the deep, rich green of groves of mango, Indian laurel, and other woods. One of the glories of the island is to be seen during the summer months, when the tree which the natives call the *flamboyan* is in blossom. It is a large and spreading tree, bearing great clusters of flowers of a brilliant red color. It blossoms profusely, and gives a strikingly gorgeous effect. The tree is quite common along the highways, many having been planted as border trees. While I failed to find the wealth of flora which I had anticipated, the color-lover will have no ground for dissatisfaction with the display which is offered along any of the Porto Rican roadways.

Guayama is another town of some antiquity, hav-

The Military Road near Ponce.

ing been founded in 1736, though its settlement antedates that period. It is a coast town practically, but it has no harbor worthy of the name. It fronts upon an open roadstead which, though well sheltered from the north, is exposed to winds from the south and southeast, under which conditions the coast reefs make it a somewhat dangerous harbor. There is a better bay at the nearby village of Arroyo, which is the usual port of entry for Guayama. The American forces, under command of General Brooke, made their landing at Arroyo, and proceeded from there to Guayama. There is little of special interest in either place. The region is one of the best sugar-raising sections of the island, and there is the usual promiscuous cultivation of small fruits and a few vegetables. Guayama boasts of the finest church edifice on the island. It has a frontage of some sixty feet, and a depth of one hundred and thirty. Its interior decorations and its altars are unusually good for so small a place. None of the churches of the island, however, are remarkably impressive. They are well constructed, and some of them are quite old, but all of them are wholly conventional in their architecture, and such artistic effect as most of them present is due rather to the decorations which time and exposure have placed upon their walls, than to any special skill of the architect.

Between Cayey and San Juan there is but one town of any note until the suburban village of Rio Piedras is reached, just outside the capital city. The location and the surroundings of this town of Caguas are admirable. In fact, it is location and surroundings which give any of these island towns their measure of attractiveness. Nature has been most lavish in her distribution of beauty spots, and man has done as much as could well be done to defile them. There is a certain picturesqueness in a thatched palm-leaf hut out in the country with a harmonious setting of banana-plants, palms, and mango-trees. But in fifty or a hundred shadeless huts grouped together in a town there is nothing save an effect of dirt and squalor. In thus clustering around a larger centre the Porto Rican displays the same gregarious tendency which leads the Chinese to live on sampans at Shanghai, and thousands of people to herd in crowded tenement-houses in New York City.

Rio Piedras is a small suburban town a few miles from San Juan. Some distinction is given it by reason of its having been, during the Spanish régime, the summer residence of the governor-general of the island. The "summer palace" is a large and rather rambling wooden structure in the rear of the cathedral, heavily shaded by trees, and presenting no special attraction except a beautifully shaded avenue running through a very badly kept rear garden. This building was placed at the disposal of, and was used by, the American army head-quarters during the weeks which preceded the evacuation of the capital.

Through all these towns there runs this splendid military road. The system by which it is maintained is admirable and effective. It is divided into sections varying from two to four or five kilometres, and each section is provided with a brick building, usually square, one story in height. These *camineros*, as they are called, are used as the dwelling-houses of peons whose business is the repairing of the roads. Each peon has his section, for which he is held responsible, and his entire time is presumably spent in supervision and repairs. Piles of broken stone are kept along the roadside, and it is the work of the peon to use this stone in the correction of any defect immediately upon its appearance. The principle employed is that excellent one of "a stitch in time." One also finds a numerous sprinkling of another pattern of "road house." These are little wayside shanties which serve their vicinity as "stores," and serve all comers who are afflicted with that kind of a thirst, with such quantity of native rum as may be desired. It is a sort of drunkard's paradise, though one rarely encounters a drunken native. Ten centavos will give any man a very long start on the road to a royal drunk. Porto Rican rum is not a safe thing for a novice to use extensively in trying chemical experiments with his internal organization. It is potent and far reaching, and I should judge that its continued use would be quite as wholesome as the use of corrosive sublimate. There is, however, a difference. There is Porto Rico rum and Porto Rico rum.

Not until the entire island shall have been equipped with a system of arterial highways approximating in their structure and their maintenance this main road from Ponce to San Juan, will Porto Rico waken to the possibilities of her resources. It is useless to produce if the cost of transportation exceeds the value of the product. The island is small, but the possibility of two or three crops a year of some of those articles which might well be among its chief products, virtually doubles or trebles a large area of its territory. Taxation of the island has been made generally unpopular because of excessive imposition. It would very likely cause much complaint and protest for the new government to impose a tax for the construction and maintenance of such a system of highways.

The present demand is rather for a relief from taxation than for the imposition of any tax beyond that

The Military Road from Ponce to San Juan.

required for the administration of affairs. Just now, public improvement is a theory, a dream, a thing for *mañana*. Roads like the one from Ponce to San Juan are wanted all over the island, but no one wants to pay for them. Probably the feeling will change when the islanders shall have had some brief breathing time and an opportunity to pull themselves together after their days of suspense and exciting change. That which is now a somewhat vague desire will become a demand which will find a ready and a cheerful response. A few months of reasonable prosperity under the conditions which will doubtless follow as a result of American control, will bring more closely home to the people their need of better highways.

IX

HIGHWAYS

An Important Factor in Island Development—Present Highway System—A Hard Journey—The Bovimotor—The Boy and the Coachman—Fun for the Boy, and Entertainment for the Audience—Porto Rican Drivers—The Need of Good Roads—Costly Transportation—A Heavy Charge on Industries.

THE development of the island of Porto Rico will depend in great measure upon the improvement of its facilities for inland transportation. The three leading cities—San Juan, Ponce, and Mayaguez—are situated on the coast. A few of the larger towns, such as Arecibo, Aguadilla, and Fajardo are similarly located. One or two, like Guayama and Humacao, may also be reckoned as coast towns. These all serve as outlets for the products of their vicinity, and receive the greater portion of their purchases from the outside world by steamer or sailing craft. The interior, and long sections of coast-line, are dependent upon pack-trains and bullock-carts. This limits production by reason of the expense of transportation, and unduly increases the cost of living, for the same reason.

The comparatively limited district reached by military roads possesses, in consequence of them, a marked advantage over other sections. Only a small portion of the island is touched by these highways. The area of the island is, approximately, 3,600 square miles. It claims but 150 miles of respectable highway. Some of this is as good as any to be found anywhere in the United States. Some of it is only fairly good, and some of it is more than doubtful. This includes what are known as the military roads. As the country is practically destitute of railway facilities, the government conceived the idea of constructing a complete system of military highways throughout the island, over which troops could be readily and speedily transferred from point to point, and out of which the officials could make a fat thing for themselves. The result was the present system—which is, by just so much, better than none at all.

Aside from this possible 150 miles, one might almost say there are no roads. There are certain narrow ways set apart for road purposes, and used for such when it is possible to use them. But they are at all times abominable, and at frequent times they are wholly impassable, even for the native bullock teams. The common service for the interior, and for many portions of the coast area, is the saddle-horse for passengers, and the mule or the pack-horse for freight. This is sometimes carried in panniers and sometimes in bulk packages, after the manner of some of our wild Rocky Mountain regions. In that country, however, the system is sometimes imperative. Here it is needless. Good roads are possible, and good roads are needed. The island produces about 30,000 tons of coffee annually. A very large percentage of this must be transported from the plantations to the shipping port in packages on the backs of mules or horses, and often over what are mere bridle-paths cut into the hill-sides. It is a laborious and expensive method of doing business, and adds unduly to the cost of the merchandise.

Aside from the question of the transportation of merchandise, there is the matter of passenger traffic. It is the affair of the people themselves if they see fit to put up with the delays, the inconveniences, and the discomforts which arise from the present custom. It is perhaps nobody's business if every Porto Rican is shaken into fragments, pounded into pulp, hampered in his business, and handicapped in the market, by reason of the roads over which he travels, or by reason of the lack of them. But the people of America have now an interest in the development of the country. A new condition has arisen. American tourists will soon be going there by hundreds and by thousands, to see the beautiful island, with its marvellously beautiful mountains and its wealth of verdure. The capitalist will go to develop its resources. The tourist cannot see the land, and the capitalist will work against heavy odds, unless there be passable roads over which the one may go for pleasure and the other for profit.

One of my many experiences over these so-called "country roads" was a journey from Ponce to Mayaguez. The distance between the two cities is not far from sixty miles. The first twenty-five miles or so, to Yauco, one covers very comfortably in an hour and a half by means of that little substitute for a railroad which runs from Ponce to Yauco. The man of the world who accepts what he finds and makes no complaint about it, will be very well satisfied with what he finds at the little Hotel Victoria in Yauco. The bed is good, the dinner is abundant and good after the manner of Spanish dinners, and the visitor will receive every possible courtesy and attention. The next morning he will start for Mayaguez, unless he wishes to spend a pleasant day in pleasant Yauco and Guanica. He may go in the saddle or by carriage. Personally, I can find no pleasure on board of a Porto Rican pony. The beasts are so small that it seems a cruelty to put even ten stone weight on their bony backs. Beyond that, it is my experience thus far that most of them give out completely after a trip of six or seven miles. Then they must either be clubbed along or lugged along.

I therefore contracted for a carriage and pair from Yauco to Mayaguez, with a relay at Sabana Grande. I reached my destination in sections. I do not know if the whole of me arrived or not. My knowledge of anatomy is too superficial to enable me to determine whether some portion of my system, conventional but not vital, does not even now dangle from some barbed-wire fence, or droop gracefully among the cocoa-nuts at the top of some tall tree along the road from Yauco to Mayaguez. As I have got along very well since that occasion, I have concluded that either the whole of me arrived, or that I can do without anything which did not come. I have had much experience with the rocky roads of the mountains of Western Carolina. I have loitered along, hub deep in the thick, black mud of Southern Illinois and of Nebraska. But for rocks, mud, and general physical discomfort, the first fifteen miles of that road from Yauco to Mayaguez can give anything of which I know in the United States ten to one, and win out in a canter. Once we mired down completely and had to be extracted by the citizens of the vicinity. The horses lost their pluck; the driver lost his temper; and I made some sacrifice of that mental placidity which is advocated by the Socratic school.

At another point I saw that any attempt to go on would only result in the utter collapse of the horses. I ordered a halt for the purpose of investigating possibilities and probabilities. While engaged in that very unsatisfactory proceeding, a beneficent Providence sent along the road a native with a pair of stout-looking black cattle with their yoke. I held up the native and made a contract with him. It resulted in the removal of the horses from the pole, and the attachment to the carriage of the black bullocks. For the greater part of the next six miles, those beasts dragged me at a snail's pace through that black and sticky mud. The spokes of the wheels were invisible, through the filling of the spaces with a solid mass of Porto Rican highway. Once or twice, at particularly treacherous-looking places, I alighted and walked through the bordering fields to avoid the risk of complete burial.

The one bright spot of that trip arose in a conversation which took place between my driver and a native boy mounted on a remarkably alert native pony. The boy and I enjoyed it. The driver did not. The lad ranged up alongside and commented unfavorably upon the driver's style and his manner of handling his team. The horses were quite used up, and the driver was nearly so. For some two miles that young rascal rode beside us and chaffed and blackguarded that driver. He paid as little heed to Jehu's voluble profanity, as he did to Jehu's efforts to lash him or his pony with what was left of Jehu's whip. He had fun with that driver. He indulged in personal remarks. He commented on the outfit, the style of the carriage, the build and the action of the horses. Jehu's wrath was unlimited, but the boy had the call on him in rapidity of motion, and the poor man was helpless. I was rather sorry when the lad fired a parting shot and turned into the yard of a wayside house. He did me good. He took me out of a despondent and muddy world and brightened the whole trip immeasurably.

Ten miles or so before reaching Mayaguez, one comes to a bit of military road, and finds a sweet and precious relief, and an opportunity to get enough of himself together to appear in human semblance on his arrival in the city. This was not my only experience, and I write from no temporary disagreement with that particular stretch of road. There are many miles like unto it, and I have traversed some of them. But they are the only thing which is to be found between the comparatively few miles of good military road and the bridle-paths of the mountains. I trust that none save the venturesome, the robust, and those in search of experiences, may be led into any attempt to travel by bridle-paths. I have tried them in the daytime, and I have tried them at night. On the whole, I think I prefer to travel over them at night. One cannot then see the difficulties and the dangers. One knows, by the position of the horse, whether he is climbing a wall or going down a precipice. He knows when his horse is floundering in a bog-hole. He knows when the horse is feeling for a foothold on the bottom of some swift and rocky stream. More than that, it is not necessary to know. The best way under such circumstances is to drop the bridle and hold the breath. One seems to have more use for breath than for bridles.

Something could be done for human comfort in a carriage-trip over these roads, if the Porto Rico drivers could be taught how to drive. They seem to have no desire or purpose except to "get there." Up hill and down, over rough and over smooth, they pound and flog their poor miserable beasts along, with never a chance to rest or breathe. Remonstrance is almost useless. Three times on my trip to Mayaguez did I get out and stand before the horses where my *cochero* could not start without running me down. On another trip of eighteen miles over the mountains, my driver used three sets of horses, and two of the pairs were utterly exhausted upon reaching the end of their short stage. Not only are better roads much needed, but better horses and better drivers are almost equally so. But the two latter are only desirable, while the first is a necessity for the commercial interests of the land.

An idea prevails very widely among many of the islanders that not only has the great government of the United States come to give them a better government, but that it has also come to give them a great many other things without their doing anything themselves. It might not be at all a bad idea to give them an object-lesson, right on the start, that would afford them a clearer comprehension of the fact that the aim of the United States Government is not so much to give everybody all he wants, or to do everything that anybody would like to have done, as it is to enable its people to get things, and to do things, for themselves. Therefore, if some fifty thousand or so of Porto Ricans could be set at work on the highways for a few weeks, under the supervision of competent engineers, it might be a valuable lesson to them, and at the same time, do something that very much needs doing.

Of course, not all roads are equally bad. Nor are the bad roads always at their worst. Something depends upon the season of the year, the wetness of the wet season, and the dryness of the dry season.

But, with the exception of the limited number of miles of military highway, I could see no evidence of any road system on the island, except that where the people wanted to go, a passage was opened and people rode over it. It must be admitted that the natural conditions of the island are generally far from being at all favorable for roadways. Along the low lands of the coast there are many long stretches of bog and swamp. These, when properly drained, make the productive cane-fields. The soil is a rich, black loam of considerable depth, which turns to a sea of mud on the slightest provocation. At present this black soil is both the bane and the blessing of the sugar planter. It makes his crop, and it also makes the mud-holes through which he must drag his crop to get it to market. As the cane is cut not far from the end of the rainy season, difficult or impassable highways are clearly a serious and expensive obstacle in the cultivation of sugar-cane. Cocoa-nuts, and a variety of small fruits, also find the most favorable conditions for their growth along these lowlands of the coast area. All are, of course, subject to the same drawback to their extensive cultivation which obtains in the case of sugar.

The mountain agriculturist is confronted with the

same general adverse conditions as those which occur in the experience of the man of the lowlands, though there are differences of detail. The soil of the mountains, generally, lends itself more readily to road construction. But in the mountains the rains are heavier and more frequent, and nothing but roads of superior construction are capable of withstanding the gullying torrents which sometimes sweep the hillsides. Throughout the major portion of the island the hill slopes are precipitous and deeply convoluted. Here and there one finds a comparatively level basin, but they are infrequent and usually of small area. Highways over the mountains would be made to best advantage by the cutting of banks or benches on the hill-sides, ascending by the easiest possible grade, and winding in and out of the coves and around the ridges to follow the convolutions. Much care would be needed, and provision for proper drainage and for bridges and culverts would be almost imperative at the inner end of the greater number of the coves.

As the lowlands make the best sugar lands, so do the hills make the best coffee section. The island should produce fifty thousand tons of coffee annually. At present the greater portion of the coffee crop is carried to the coast in packs on the little island ponies. The difference in cost of transporting fifty

Where the Natives Live.

thousand tons of coffee alone, by this method, and of carrying by wagon over a good road, would, in a few years pay for scores of miles of suitable roadway. The mountain district of the island may be safely estimated at three-fourths of the entire area.

Of this territory, probably not more than five per cent. is under cultivation for commercial or market purposes. Some portion of it is, of course, unsuitable for agricultural purposes, and could only be used for grazing. A small percentage would be unavailable for any purpose. This limited cultivation is in a measure due to the lack of energy and ambition on the part of the native people. But beyond that and operating as a factor in the apathy of the natives, has always stood the lack of encouragement to greater activity. The difficulty and the undue cost of transportation of products, have acted in some cases as a limiting force, and in many cases as a wholly prohibitive force.

The people of the island have been heavily taxed for road construction, but the roads for which they have paid have not been built. One will often hear the remark through the country, that if they had all for which they have paid, the highways would be paved with gold. No repetition of this process is at all needed. The United States have assumed control of the island with an assurance of the beginning of a new order of things. One of the planks in the Porto Rico platform is relief from political oppression and from the robbery, through taxation, of which the island people have been made the victims. We have plenty of honest and skilful engineers. If it were possible for us to send some of them to Porto Rico to supervise the work and the expenditure involved in the construction of an adequate system of roads and highways, it would be a most excellent investment for the island to borrow a suitable sum of money for such a purpose. The island is now wholly free from debt. Financial obligation, *per se*, is no advantage to any country. Good roads are an imperative need in the development of Porto Rico. The assumption of a few millions of dollars of obligation, to be honestly expended in highway construction, would be an excellent and profitable investment rather than a debt. State roads are rapidly growing in favor here in the United States where their construction is a convenience and a desirability. In Porto Rico, the position goes beyond either of those points, and places good roads in the list of absolute necessities. Without them, a vast area of our new possession remains an uncultivated wilderness. With them, hundreds of thousands of acres can be utilized as profitably productive farms and plantations.

X

RAILROADS AND TELEGRAPHS

The Railways of To-day—The Ponce and Yauco Division—The Humiliation of a Traveller—The Solitary Occupant of the Apartment of the First Class—Familiar Sights in a Foreign Land—The Requirements of the Island—Present System of Transportation—Probable Benefits of Railway Extension—The United States in the Telegraph Business—Cable Lines.

A FEW years ago the island of Porto Rico passed through a spasm of desire for progress and development. I have been unable to learn positively whether the scheme for the construction of a railroad was originated and developed by the people of the island for their general benefit, or whether it was the work of the particular set of officials who were then engaged in the process of making a fortune out of the island within the briefest possible time. But whatever the source of the idea, a railroad was projected which should encircle the island. Work was begun at different points, and the result of the work is manifest to-day in the shape of three short stretches of what passes for a railroad, and sundry officials whose financial status was decidedly bettered by the enterprise. It is claimed that there are now one hundred and forty-three miles of railroad in operation, with one hundred and seventy miles under construction. Those in operation include the line from Ponce to Yauco, on the south coast; the line from Hormigueros to Aguadilla, passing through Mayaguez, on the west coast; and the line which runs westward from San Juan, through Bayamon and Arecibo, to Camuy, on the northern coast. These are all single-track roads, and of narrow gauge. The equipment is decidedly primitive, and the whole affair strikes an American as being rather toy-like.

Taking these outlines in more accurate detail, the statement would be as follows:

The Ponce and Yauco division shows twenty-six miles of main track, and passes through the villages of Guayanilla and Tallaboa. The line from Hormigueros to Aguadilla covers a fraction of over forty-three miles of main track, and includes the city of Mayaguez, and the towns of Añasco, Rincón, and Aguada, along its route. From San Juan to Camuy the line is seventy-four and one-third miles. Its principal stations are Bayamon and Arecibo, though it includes some half dozen more of less importance. There is a line of some sixteen miles running from San Juan, through Rio Piedras, to Carolina. There is also a steam tram-line running from San Juan to the suburban town of Rio Piedras. This is now said to be in the hands of Chicago parties.

My first experience with this railway system will serve as a fair illustration of the probable experience of any travellers whose good fortune enables them to exchange the miseries of a carriage journey around the island, for the greater comfort of a railway trip over a portion of the route. My objective point was Mayaguez, and I decided to experiment in Porto Rican railways to the extent of a trip to Yauco, the termination of the road in the direction in which I wished to go. On the southern border of the city of Ponce, a few rods back from the highway, one sees a rusty-looking building, of two stories in height, with a half-effaced "Ponce" painted upon the end toward the roadway. An investigation will reveal some grass-covered tracks and sundry boxes on small wheels which an active imagination will turn into freight-cars. A further exercise of the imaginative faculty enables one to determine that he is at the Ponce station of the *Compañia de los Ferrocarriles de Puerto Rico*. Doors facing upon the grass-grown trackway bear the following signs: *Ynspeccion, Telegrafo, Oficina,* and *Equipages*. The apartment designated as *Equipages*, is evidently the waiting-room, and in one corner of it a window is indicated as the ticket-officer by means of a sign marked, *Despacho de*

Billetes. As I had never seen any sign of a moving or a waiting train about the station during any of my frequent journeys past the building, it seemed necessary to obtain some information regarding time-tables.

I pegged away at my Spanish until I had evolved a sentence which seemed of admirable construction and entire correctness. At the station I found a man who wore an official cap and a pleasant smile. He wore other things also, but those were the most noticeable. I faced him and proceeded to unload my specimen of pure Castilian. "*Que hora el tren para Yauco?*" said I. I considered this as a masterpiece. *Por* means "for," but had I said *por Yauco* it would, in that connection, have meant "through Yauco," a feat which was beyond the immediate possibilities of the *Compañia de los Ferrocarriles de Puerto Rico*, a title which rather overweights the outfit. Therefore *para* was the word, and I was proud of my accomplishments. But my pride took the usual tumble. The genial official looked at me even more genially, and replied: "'E goes to Yauco at 'alf pas' four." "The deuce he does," said I. "Look here, old chap, your English seems to be an improvement on my Spanish. Therefore, with your kind permission, we will conduct our further negotiations in the tongue which will soon become the established language of this beautiful island." I fancy that this peroration rather floored him, but he grinned very genially, and we resorted to a compound of American and Spanish monosyllables, and got along beautifully.

As there was no " 'alf pas' four " until the following day, I had ample time to prepare my mind and my simple luggage for the journey of thirty-five kilometres from Ponce to Yauco. Shortly before the appointed hour, I found what was called the *tren* standing on the grass-plot in front of the station. It consisted of two or three diminutive freight-cars, a toy mail-car, and a couple of coaches of about the size of an American street-car. The whole was drawn by a toy locomotive. As a piece of mechanical skill, the engine was open to little criticism. So far as its working parts were visible, they presented every evidence of being of the first class. It was of solid and substantial structure, and of an English pattern, though, I think, of Spanish make. The gauge of the track is three feet eleven and a quarter inches.

One of the coaches was marked III. The other was divided into two compartments, one finished in plain wood, and marked II., the other upholstered with leather, and marked I. The numerals indicated the class. The third-class car was soon filled by the waiting passengers. Evidently the third-class is the popular and common mode of travel. The second-class compartment held four American soldiers, who paid no fare. The imposing first-class compartment held one American newspaper man and his gripsack. The newspaper man regretted his ignorant act, and trembled lest he be charged with ostentation. But one American dollar for a railway trip of an hour and a half does not strike an unsophisticated American newspaper man as wildly extravagant—if his paper pays the bill.

The train tore on its way at the frightful speed of some sixteen miles an hour. The road runs through beautiful country. It is not easy to find any country here that is not beautiful. The line follows the coast generally. Upon one side were frequent views of the ocean, and upon the other a constant panorama of exquisitely beautiful mountain scenery, with the rich lights and shades of the evening sun resting on the wrinkled sides of the hills. The road-bed is fairly good, and the well-built culverts, where the line crosses the little streams, might well be imitated by many a railroad in the States. We ran past acres of sugar-cane, and stopped at two little villages—Tallaboa and Guayanilla. The engine-whistle screamed at curves and crossings with all the vigor of which it was capable, and with a volume and tone which suggested those boyish instruments of ear-torture which I used to make in days of youth out of an empty tomato-can and waxed cord. I believe they were called, very appropriately, "devil's fiddles." I got rather tired of that engine-whistle, and beg to refer the operators of the road to some of the statistics, which show the cost of the locomotive whistle through the waste of steam.

In spite of the wide difference in environment, and in the difference of my mechanical and social surroundings, I think that no other experience on the island quite took me back to America as did that little run on that pocket edition of a railroad. At the little stations at which we stopped there was the same group of curious idlers, the "committee of the unemployed," gathered as self-appointed delegates to "see the train come in," that will be found around the depot of any country town in America. At Yauco, a large percentage of the population had gathered for the same purpose. Friends greeted the friends who arrived, and the idlers gaped and stared in the most conventional manner of their kind. A horde of urchins and a few of larger growth clamored for the chance of earning a few centavos by carrying one's satchels to house or hotel. There was the familiar centrifugal movement of the crowd as the train pulled in, the familiar thronging about the steps as the passengers alighted, and the usual reflux and dispersion immediately following. But the vision faded as I made my way to the hotel, and disappeared utterly when I entered it.

Porto Rico needs a proper railway system, and it needs American capital and American brains to build it. The first company in the field is likely to hold a monopoly, as a district which is hardly half the size of the State of New Jersey does not present unlimited chances for competition. It is therefore quite desirable that such an enterprise be essayed by bona-fide operators, and that no franchise be granted to those whose aim is purely speculative, and who are unsupported by the actual cash capital necessary for construction and operation. The amount required would not be large, from the stand-point of American railway investments, and the returns would doubtless be ample. Some four to five hundred miles of track are all that would be necessary, and perhaps all that would be desirable, at present. The belt line should be completed. It would draw from and supply the lowland border of the coast line, and by doing so greatly economize in the expense of marketing the sugar crop, which is the principal industry of that region. It would also open many possibilities in the direction of other agricultural industries. It would connect a considerable number of the principal towns and cities, and so facilitate the exchange of commodities locally. The present sys-

RAILROADS AND TELEGRAPHS 143

tem is by means of a small steamer which has been wont to circle the island, stopping at a regular line of ports. Its trips, though continuous, were necessarily infrequent, and, for passengers, often too tardy for satisfactory service. In a trip from San Juan to Ponce, the choice lies between a drive of a hundred miles across the island, or the water journey around it. The drive is made, with relays, in about fourteen hours. The cost, before the arrival of the Americans, is said to have been sixteen pesos, or about ten dollars, according to the rate of exchange. Americans, all of whom were evidently regarded as the possessors of more money than was good for them, were charged from thirty to forty pesos for the trip.

Fourteen hours in a carriage is a hard and tiring journey even over that best of roads from San Juan to Ponce. The alternative was the water journey, which might take two days or more. This, in pleasant weather, is a charming little voyage if one is in no hurry, and is a good sailor. But the weather is not always pleasant, the sea is not always smooth, and one is sometimes in something of a hurry, even in Porto Rico. Under the present system, there is no such thing as prompt delivery of goods from place to place on the island, unless it happen that a steamer is about to start for the point to which the goods are to go. Manifestly, both travel, and foreign and domestic traffic, are heavily handicapped through lack of railroad facilities.

The belt line, with its deviations from the direct course in order to strike certain points which should be included in its route, would measure not far from three hundred and fifty miles. It should be under that rather than above it. Another line is needed quite as much as this, if not more. The coast cities and towns can be reached, in many cases, by the water route. They are much less cut off than are the inland points. Therefore, this other line should cross the island from east to west, bisecting it as equally as the topography of the region will permit. The ground has already been looked over by competent authority, and a route has been partially determined which is pronounced wholly feasible. Such a route should have its western terminus at Mayaguez, run from there northeast to Lares, and from Lares eastward to touch the best possible coast point by the way of Caguas or Cayey. This, with the belt-line, would run three generally parallel tracks across the island from east to west, with a north and south track at each end. As the island is something less than forty miles in average width, such a system would bring any and all parts of it within, generally, ten miles of a railroad. Branch lines could be run to points which promised a paying traffic.

The motive power might be either steam or electricity, according to the economy of the one or the other for the amount of business to be done. Whether any or all of it would prove financially profitable is largely a matter of speculation. The construction of such a system would open up hundreds of thousands of acres of available land, and greatly enhance the value of real estate without necessarily greatly increasing the cost of it to immediate purchasers. The prices already asked for the land seem far beyond a reasonable valuation under the present conditions. The railway would turn what now seems a fictitious value into an actual value. This system may seem over-extensive for the island. It probably is for the immediate time. But in just so far as it is carried out, the resources of the island will be given opportunity for development. Unless it is done, Porto Rico is quite likely to stay where it now is—a rich garden, uncultivated, neglected, wasted.

The cost of construction of such a railway is a matter for the determination of experts. Most of the coast line would run over fairly level land, but some bridging and some fills would be needed. Ballasting would be required in some of the boggy and swampy land, but an ample supply of rock is readily available. Some skilful engineering work would be required for the middle, or mountain, line. There are ranges to be crossed at considerable altitudes, and many of the gaps could only be reached by devious climbing up the precipitous hill-sides. All cost of operations would best be estimated on an American basis, plus the cost of transportation. Labor is abundant, and it should be cheap; but its nominal cost would be enhanced by reason of its inefficiency. A dozen or two of experienced American section hands would do the work of several scores of jabbering Porto Rican peons, who have not been trained to regular and persistent work. Rails would have to be sent out, though there is a considerable stock already piled up for a track which is said to be "under construction." It is probable that there would be an advantage in sending out cross-ties and bridge timbers. There is wood on the island, but the greater portion of it is either unsuitable, or else is too valuable for such purposes.

I am unable to say in just whose hands the ownership of the present incomplete system rests. The contract for its construction was given to a French company, but if there was not some kind of a "stand in" on the part of Spanish officials, it was an unusual piece of Spanish official conduct. This contract, I am told, was once annulled because of the failure of the contractors to fulfil the terms of the agreement. The matter was patched up, probably by the use of a little golden solder. It might be possible for American investors to obtain this charter and the railroad property at a reasonable price. Failing that, or failing to oblige the present company to fulfil its contract with due promptness, it might be advisable to run a new road wholly independent of the old. The matter of the "inherent righteousness" of such a proceeding might lie in a question of equity, or it might lie in the question of the honest act and intention of the present owners.

The island is supplied with a fairly effective telegraph system, which extends to all the principal towns and cities. Its methods and appliances are not entirely up to date, but it has answered all purposes. The property belonged to and was maintained by the government. Private messages were accepted and forwarded at a fixed tariff, though government or official messages were given precedence over all private or commercial communications. With the transfer of the island, the system passes into the hands of the United States Government. I encountered a somewhat unique complaint regarding the line after it had come into the hands of the American officials. It was made by a leading merchant of Mayaguez, and was to the effect that while the wires were open to the public, as they had formerly been, and every possible courtesy was extended, the public was not allowed to pay for the transmission of despatches. The ground of this unusual kind of objection lay in the fact that, because of this courtesy and gratuitous accommodation, merchants felt reluctant to use the wires as freely as they wished and as freely as they would if they had been allowed to pay for the service. I think the trouble has now been remedied.

A good deal of damage was done to the system by the Spanish troops as they fell back across the island. Wires were cut and poles were thrown down. As the American forces moved forward, the damages were repaired by the Signal Corps of our army. There has been a pronounced objection in many quarters in the United States to the government ownership of telegraph lines, but the fates have decreed that, for a time at least, the United States Government shall be the proprietor of some five hundred miles of telegraph line with some fifty or more offices in different parts of the island. The submarine telegraph system is controlled by the West India and Panama Telegraph Company, which operates under a contract having several years yet to run. The cable service of the island is a monopoly. With a half-built and wholly inadequate railway service, a government ownership of the local telegraph line and a foreign monopoly of the cable connection, some interesting problems are presented in the departments of railways and telegraphs in Porto Rico.

XI

INDUSTRIAL POSSIBILITIES

Our New Farm—Mining Possibilities and Timber Lands—The Outlook for Sugar—The Coffee Industry—Encouragement in Tobacco-growing—Obstacles to Export Fruit Trade—Cattle-raising—An American Bermuda—Victims of Manana.

PORTO RICO is evidently a farm, and not a workshop. Its resources are almost exclusively agricultural. There is a theory of mining possibilities, but thus far I have been unable to find any foundation for it. What foundation there is seems to lie in two directions. One of these appears in the old tales of nearly four hundred years ago, when the discoverers of the island and its early settlers claimed the new possession as a land of gold. The other appears in the old saying that "the wish is the father of the thought." If there be gold there, it seems strange that four hundred years of hunger for the yellow metal should not have established the fact of its presence beyond all doubt. Iron is there, and also copper and galena. But until these metals become less readily and less economically available in scores of other places, there is little to encourage investment in their development in Porto Rico. Still, mining possibilities are always questions for determination by mining experts, and valuable properties may even yet be found to exist on the island.

There is little encouragement in timber. There are some fine woods on the island, but the commercial supply is very limited. The area throughout which such woods are to be found is of comparatively small extent, and is exceedingly rough in character. A moderate amount of highly valuable timber might be got out at a reasonable cost, but the greater portion of what there is is of mountain growth, and its removal would involve the construction of roads or logways through a country which is even rougher than our Southern mountains. Some logs can and will be taken out at profitable prices, but there is hardly enough of timber-land to make any very extensive business.

It is chiefly to the cultivation of the rich and fertile soil of the island that we must look for its industrial wealth. There we enter a promising field. Sugar, coffee, and tobacco are now its principal products, with rum and Porto Rico molasses as important by-products. At present sugar-raising is a somewhat doubtful enterprise. The low price of raw sugar during recent years has caused the suspension of operations on a large number of plantations in different parts of the island. The possibility of cane-raising at a profit under the conditions likely to be presented by the market for some time to come is an open question. How much might be accomplished by the application of thoroughly systematic business methods upon the plantation, I am unable to say. That does not seem to be a common practice. It may be that Porto Rican sugar has seen its best days. There are other lands in which the cane is produced with less of labor and less of risk than in Porto Rico.

Weather conditions sometimes interfere to the serious injury or loss of crops. Different conditions during the same year may be presented in different parts of the island. There may be excessive rains or excessive drought in certain portions, while in other portions the conditions may be entirely favorable. Many acres of sugar land of excellent quality can be bought.

Out of some of them good money could doubtless be made by the application of good business methods and the adoption of the best of modern machinery. But the investment is too speculative for any save those who fully understand the work, and who are possessed of capital enough for its successful prosecution. The business requires considerable capital, as each plantation should operate its own mill, and an area of land must be cultivated which will warrant the erection and operation of the mill. The percentage of saccharine matter carried by Porto Rican cane is said to be high, and it is possible that this percentage, backed by the most effective machinery obtainable, might equalize or more than equalize the advantages presented in cane-growth in other districts. An economy for all sugar plantations will be effected by the construction of an improved highway system, and the introduction of the belt-line railroad around the island, by which the present expensive system of hauling the sugar to export points on the coast would be greatly modified. There are few lines of business that will warrant the hauling of a product on slow-moving bullock-teams, over miles of rocks or through miles of mud. An improvement in transportation facilities may mean the salvation of many acres of sugar lands.

Porto Rico now produces from twenty-five to thirty thousand tons of coffee annually. Very little of this comes to the United States, and few of us have any idea of the excellence of the Porto Rican product. The finest grade is consumed on the European continent. Most of the inferior grades are sent to Cuba. European prices are about the same as the price on the Java article. The great majority of American coffee-drinkers are content with the cheaper coffee which is obtained chiefly from the lowlands of South America. Those who are more particular about their palates sip from the fragrant cup a decoction which they firmly believe has come from the Persian Gulf or from far-famed Java. But "Mocha" and "Java" are now little more than trade terms for coffee of certain kinds rather than for coffee from certain localities. Most of that which we drink under those very respectable old titles, comes to us from the mountain districts of South America. Those who may be disposed to question this statement are referred to the custom-house reports for recent years, where they will find statements to show the quantity which we have imported of genuine Mocha and Java within the last ten years or so. They may then calculate how far that quantity would go in filling the demand.

Lowland coffee yields more abundantly, but yields an inferior article. Upland, or hill-grown coffee is less prolific, but its quality is superior. The Porto Rican coffee is all hill grown. The principal coffee district is among the hills of the western third of the island. The conditions there are particularly favorable for its production. Coffee raising is a profitable industry. At least, I have yet to see a coffee-planter who was not in comfortable circumstances, and many of them are rich. Of course, there are those of small

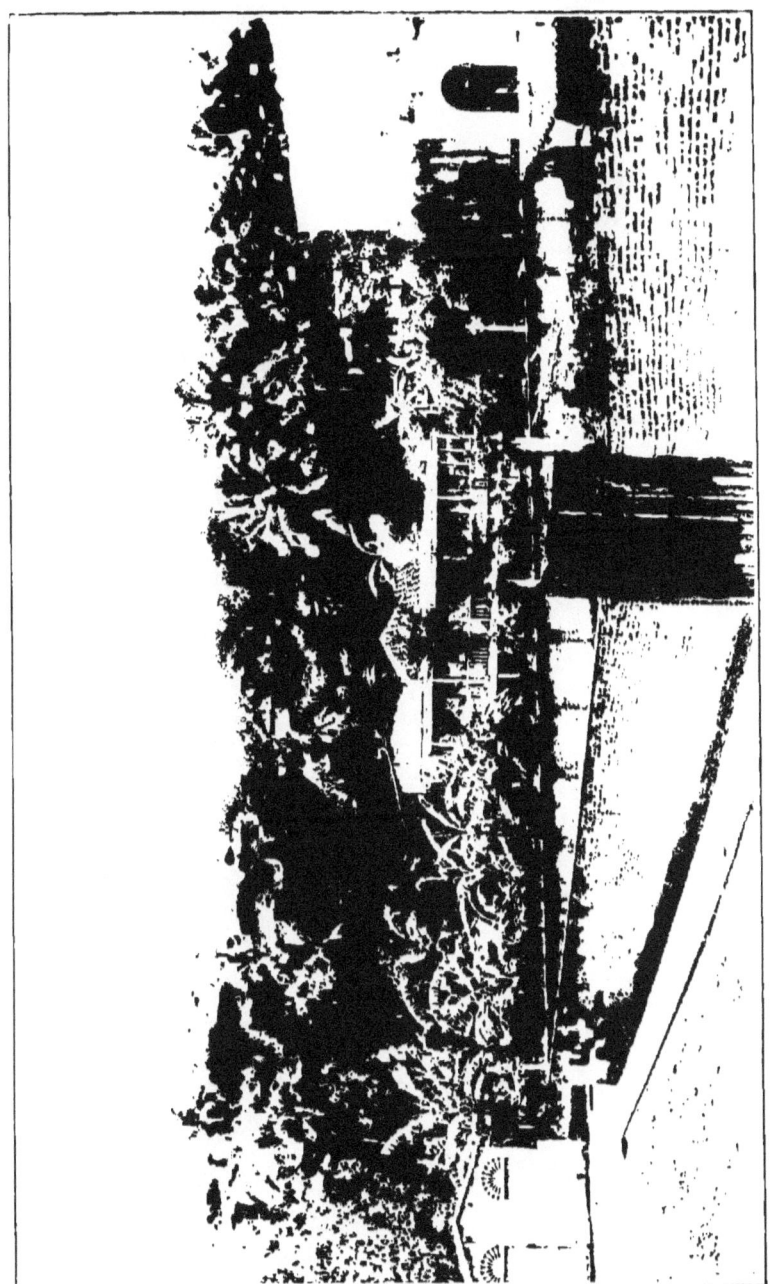

The Home of a Planter.

possessions who raise a little coffee, men of an acre or two of ground in the coffee district. But they are not regarded as coffee planters. Coffee-planting as a business means a plantation with several hundred acres under cultivation. Then it pays. There is room for some extension of the industry, though I am told by one whose information I regard as wholly competent, that it is very doubtful if the entire crop which the island could be made to produce would much more than double the present output.

But coffee raising is no more a bonanza than is sugar raising. High winds may shake the berries from the plants, and may even play havoc with the entire plantation. Constant watchfulness must be maintained, and much careful and diligent work expended. The plants must be pruned to prevent an overgrowth which would cause deterioration of the quality of the berry, and increase the labor and difficulty of gathering. The industry requires either a considerable capital or a number of years of growth from a comparatively small investment. In either case time is involved. Nursery slips of a year's growth are set out to form the plantation, and two years are required before bearing. The plant reaches its full bearing at about the fifth year, and its life of service covers about twenty years. Neither sugar nor coffee appears to be a business for small farmers. The attempt has been made to encourage the cultivation of cane on small plantations, by the erection of central mills operated on the general business plan of the country creamery in the United States. But these have not resulted in any marked success, and some have been complete failures. This is probably due in large measure to the lack of energy and ambition on the part of the small proprietors in the vicinity of the mills. Small plantings of coffee might be depended on as a "cash crop," serving the same purpose as the little cotton patch of many of the negroes of the Southern States. In coffee, as in sugar, it would appear that the average small planter does not find enough need for cash to induce him to do a little work to get it.

Another possible industry presents itself in the cultivation of tobacco. Thousands of acres of land are entirely suitable for this crop, and a considerable business is already done. I am told by tobacco dealers in this country that the Porto Rican leaf has but little standing here. It was my own experience as a smoker, and that of scores of other Americans with whom I discussed the topic, that certain brands of Porto Rico cigars made a very satisfactory smoke, while the majority could only be classified as vile. There was little evidence of any effort to do anything more with the native tobacco than to plant it, let it grow, and after a crude process of curing, to make it up into a crude cigar, or into the cigarettes which the natives consume in vast quantity. It was also sold in long ropy "plugs" in stores and at the market-places. The prevailing idea among the American visitors was that if certain varieties of leaf were planted and properly cultivated, a profitable industry could readily be established. It was also thought that if a properly cured leaf were made into cigars, in a proper manner, the result would be a superior and readily salable article. The tobacco of the island has a distinct flavor of its own, which would prove wholly acceptable to a large number of users of the weed.

The people of the island claim that much of their best tobacco now goes to Cuba, where it is manufactured, and shipped to the United States as a high grade of Cuban product. I can see no reason to believe that any special effort has been made toward the development of the Porto Rican weed to its highest stage of perfection, and I can see no reason to doubt that business intelligence applied to tobacco culture and manufacture on the island will some day make Porto Rican cigars a choice article for the American smoker. As it is now, one may buy there, for two and a half to three dollars a hundred, cigars which average on an equality with those which retail in the States at three for a quarter. But they are not well made or well finished, and the tobacco itself is but poorly cultivated and indifferently cured. I am well satisfied that thousands of acres of the rich soil could be made immensely profitable by the cultivation of tobacco for high-grade cigars.

The possibilities of an export trade in fruits and vegetables is a somewhat complicated question. Cocoa-nuts, bananas, mangoes, pineapples, and all tropical fruits grow, or can be made to grow, in abundance. The difficulty with the more prominent of these is along the line of competition with strongly established concerns now drawing their supplies from other sources. Operators already engaged in the fruit business have their connection for supply, and their channels for outlet, already determined and well in hand. They own warehouses and steamships adapted and constructed for their business. Large capital would probably be required to obtain an equal footing in the home market for fruit, in competition with the older houses. In pineapples, there would come the competition with a rapidly extending industry in Florida, which has a manifest advantage in facility for reaching the market. Oranges and grape-fruit offer encouraging prospects. The oranges already grown under no careful cultivation, are of a quality and size which insures a superior fruit if better cared for. The crop would be wholly safe from danger or frost, and though no more of a "sure thing" than any other industry, here or there, the outlook for prospective orange growers is highly encouraging.

There are also many possibilities in vegetable gardening. The possibility of several crops a year would seem to mark the region as one eminently favorable for vegetable canning. There is no natural reason why Porto Rico should not be an American Bermuda for the production of such vegetables as are now imported from that island. It might also prove a serious competitor for Florida in winter garden products. The climate and general conditions of life in Porto Rico would be more agreeable than those of Southern Florida. The present system of market gardening is not clearly indicative of the possibilities of the island. It is, however, a fair inference that if present results can be attained by present methods, the application of intelligent and careful methods under a systematic management would produce a far more desirable result. To such an improvement obstacles are presented in two directions. There is little to encourage a belief that the native people will be disposed to make a radical change in their nature and habits, and transform themselves from a lazy, easy-going, and, in the main, idle people, into active and energetic workers. On the other hand, there is little encouragement for active and energetic workers to go to the island. Their success and prosperity would be too greatly dependent upon a sufficient general extension of special industries to offer much inducement for emigration.

The raising of beef cattle may also be included among the possible industries. The breed already raised upon the island is of good quality, though of no more than an ordinary size. The average weight will probably be not far from eleven hundred to thirteen hundred pounds. Large areas in the interior could be utilized for cattle-raising, and there are tracts along the coast-lands which would be more readily available for this purpose than for any other. Pork and pork products are imported in important quantity, and there should be a promising opportunity for a limited number to engage in hog-raising. Range land in the interior could be obtained at reasonable prices and the animals turned loose upon it to feed on plantains and edible roots. Corn, for fattening, grows readily throughout the island.

Of mechanical industry there is now little or nothing. It is doubtful if the local market is large enough to warrant any extensive industry in any line. Raw materials for almost any business would have to be imported, and the education of a race to persistent day in and day out labor, would be no simple matter. Most of the industry with which the native people have been at all acquainted, has been of a nature which permitted them to consult their personal inclinations to a considerable extent. The tones of the mandate which implies man's starvation if he will not work are but feebly heard in Porto Rico, and nature weakens the force of even so much of it as may be heard, by a lavish bounty which reduces the necessity for work to its minimum. Even those who go to the island, either in search of a livelihood or for fortune-making, will speedily fall into the ways of the place and, more or less consciously, adopt the local *mañana* as an object of worship. Porto Rico will be developed—some time, but its development is far from likely to proceed at a pace which will at all rival the growth of our Western States. If we must have outlying islands, Porto Rico is one of the best and most promising that could be had at all.

Whatever may be the result of increased contact between these people and ourselves, however much or little they may adopt of American customs and habits in many things which are now widely different, one thing is quite certain, and that is that any settlers on the island will soon drop into the prevalent indolence. It is in the air and in the life. For a time it is possible to fight it, but the conviction grows that ultimately one must yield to it, and accept *mañana* as the law of life. It is not the intense heat, for, measured by the thermometer, the heat is not so very intense, and in most places it is tempered by a breeze which elsewhere would doubtless be refreshing. But it is hardly so there. The air is dull and heavy, and one grows listless. Physical exertion of any kind becomes a bore, and mental exertion becomes almost an impossibility. How it would be if one could get a restful sleep I cannot say. I regret that I have not been able to try that. In the hotel sleeping-dungeon, one lies and stifles until he rouses in the morning, unrested and unrefreshed. The very necessary mosquito-canopy excludes any air which may be in circulation with the impenetrability of sheet-iron, while it is no more effective against mosquitoes than a barbed-wire fence would be. One might in time become used to it all and find life there as pleasant as it is anywhere. But before he reaches that point he will land in the clutches of potent, implacable, irresistible *mañana*. With an income, a comfortable home, and nothing to do, Porto Rico is on the borders of Lotus Land.

XII

COMMERCE ON THE ISLAND

Ephemeral Trade—Problems for the Merchants—Arrival of the Commercial Army—Disappointed Speculators and Promoters—Local Productions—The Volume of Imports—The Export Trade—Porto Rican Business Methods—Influence of Tariff—Outlook for Americans.

FOR the first two or three weeks of our occupation of a part of the island, business was a secondary consideration. Everybody was having a kind of holiday, except the hundreds of laborers, truckmen, and boatmen, for whom our operations furnished abundant employment. The majority had their attention and interest divided by novel and stirring scenes. It was a time of excitement. Troops of cavalry, artillery, and infantry were coming and going in every direction. The streets were filled with sight-seers, and business men stood in their shop-doors to watch the little military drama which was being played for their benefit. During this period certain lines of business experienced an unprecedented activity. The demand for eatables and for drinkables was something beyond Porto Rican ideas. Pedlers of fruit, cakes, and home-made confectionery (save the mark) appeared by the score. They came in swarms and droves. They pervaded the city and the camps. But that is not business.

After the first days of turmoil things began to settle a little. Shoppers, soldiers and sailors, officers and men, newspaper correspondents, and a few other civilians, filled the stores in search of curios and mementos, and for the purpose of replenishing wardrobes. That meant many sales and many pesos in Porto Rican cash-boxes. But even that was not business. It represented only a brief and temporary condition. The rush of it was soon over, and the dispersion of troops to other points left Porto Rico to settle still farther into its usual state. The settling process continued with the return of troops to the States, and matters rapidly dropped into the normal groove. Merchants looked over stocks depleted through several months of uncertain political and commercial conditions, and considered their replenishment.

The first problem was the cheapest market in which to place their orders, and there came a trouble. The cheapest market to-day might be the dearest to-morrow. A merchant might place an order for domestics in Manchester, and an order for cutlery in Elberfeld, only to find, upon the arrival of the goods, that the wares which B, his neighbor, had ordered a few days later from New York enabled B to sell at less than A's cost price, with ample margin of profit to B. The gates to the Porto Rican merchant's millennium were not immediately opened to him, and he groped in outer darkness, hoping for a ray of light, and grumbling at the new government which hid it from him.

The question was one of tariff rates, and no man knew what would be done about them. For many weeks matters remained in this uncertain state, and there was much of serious complaint among the local merchants. They wanted goods and were quite ready to buy them, but the question of the proper market in which to make their purchases hinged on the action of the American Government. If Porto Rico were to be given a territorial form of government, with free exchange of commodities with the United States, American wares would present economic advantages over goods from Europe. If some special arrangement were made for our new possessions, and a general tariff applied to all imports, the advantage, on some lines, would lie with European manufactures. Orders for goods were held back, and merchants felt that they were losing opportunities.

This tariff question presented itself also as an impediment to the operations of American business men. American commerce followed sharply upon the heels of the American army. Within two weeks of the military occupation of the island, a steamer arrived out bringing the advance guard of the commercial army. The first to land was the representative of a large tobacco establishment. The second represented a brewery. On the same steamer came a little bunch of general prospectors, and a group of men interested in railway contracts. The tobacco man stayed, and the beer man stayed, and both did a fairly satisfactory business. The general prospectors talked much of the value of real estate and the possibility of speculation. Then they went home. The railroad men surveyed the situation from the stand-points of the Hotel Français and the Ponce plaza, and packed their grips for a return by the first steamer. The closing days of August brought other steamers. All carried as many passengers as their cabin accommodations would permit. Among them were a few whose aims were wholly legitimate and whose journey was warranted. Some of these were representatives of reliable houses who had come for general information regarding a market for their particular wares. Few of them saw much encouragement, and most of them returned by the first boat they could catch.

The great majority of the arrivals consisted of the

purely speculative element. Very many of them were young men who had just about enough money to get them out, to keep them on the island for a week or two, and to get them home again. Those who were wise went home as soon as they could. The prominence given to the island of Porto Rico during the early months of 1898, and much talk of its importance as a strategic point, and of its richness and fertility, would seem to have greatly magnified the spot in the minds of the general American public, both with regard to its area and its commercial importance. The long months of talking and planning for the invasion and conquest of the island, and the great army which it was proposed to send there appear to have given a decidedly mistaken and exaggerated idea regarding the entire situation.

In comparative figures, Porto Rico is less than half the size of the State of New Jersey. It would take about fourteen Porto Ricos to cover the State of New York. Three Rhode Islands would cover Porto Rico and leave enough margin for a foot-path around it. Less than one hundred miles will measure its length, and less than forty miles, its width. We have but one or two States in the Union so densely populated as Porto Rico. Its average to the square mile exceeds that of Connecticut, New York, or New Jersey, and far exceeds that of Ohio or Illinois. It is not a wild, new country for commercial or speculative exploitation. Its settlement antedates that of America. San Juan had been established for more than fifty years when Menendez built his fort at St. Augustine, and had seen twenty different governors of the island before Virginia Dare was born.

Yet with all this comparative density of population, with all the richness of the soil of the island, with a people whose numbers are but a little less than those who make their homes in Brooklyn, the entire trade of the island, domestic and foreign, export and import, is less than that of many an American city with one-tenth of its number of inhabitants. A notable discrepancy arises in the figures given for the exports and imports. This is partly due to the difficulty of obtaining accurate statistics, and partly to the complication of the terms "dollars" and "pesos." The terms are often made interchangeable, but the coins are not, except at variable rates of exchange which makes it difficult to convert the one into the other with any accuracy. In the following schedule, the values are represented in American dollars.

The local trade in local products is chiefly confined to the morning market for table supplies, which is held in all the cities and larger towns. The total imports and exports hardly reach a gross amount of thirty millions of dollars a year, and the imports exceed the exports by a couple of millions. I have been unable to find any statistics which I was willing to accept as wholly reliable. So far as I can learn, no complete report has been submitted by the United States consul, and there are discrepancies which I cannot reconcile in the published reports of the English consul and those of the Dutch consul. I can, therefore, only give figures which are approximate, though they are sufficiently close for general purposes.

Cotton goods appear to be the largest item among the imports, and they represent a trade of two or three millions of dollars, varying from year to year, according to the prices and the success or failure of the crop products of the island. Rice is imported to the value of one and a half to two millions of dollars. Flour, chiefly from the United States, approximates three-quarters of a million dollars. Dried, salt, and pickled fish, of which Canada seems to obtain the lion's share of the trade, represents a million to a million and a quarter. The United States has the major portion of a trade in pork and pork products, which about equals the fish business. Woollen goods are, naturally, of but limited consumption in so warm a climate, and the trade is probably less than $150,000 in amount. Agricultural implements represent a business of three to four hundred thousand dollars. Boots and shoes, almost exclusively from Spain, represent some five or six hundred thousand. Chinaware, glassware, lumber, coal, soap, furniture, and other articles of general use and consumption represent amounts varying from one to three or four hundred thousand dollars.

The most astonishing thing in the whole list of importations is the item of vegetable and garden products. These are imported into that country, which is in itself but a natural garden, in which can and should be raised every form of vegetable necessary or desirable for consumption, and the annual value of the imports approximates $400,000, and the weight 7,000 tons. The island uses $150,000 worth of imported candles and $50,000 worth of imported butter yearly. It uses two to three hundred thousand dollars' worth of cheese, of which the Netherlands have, for the last few years, furnished much the greater part. Uruguay and the Argentine supply it with one to three thousand tons of jerked beef annually. Wine, beers, and liquors take something more than a half a million a year out of the country.

Among Porto Rican exports coffee is the heaviest item. This reaches an average valuation of some $8,000,000 a year. Sugar ranks next, and approximates three to four million dollars. Tobacco goes to the extent of some half a million, and molasses touches about the same figure. Hides, cattle, timber, and fruit are represented in the list, but their value is comparatively inconsiderable. Guano, to the extent of half a million a year, appears in the reports for some years; but I am unable to account for either the article or the amount. Some corn has been sent to Cuba, some native rum to Spain, and some bay rum to France and to the United States.

It will thus be seen that, as yet, the island offers but a comparatively limited amount of business, either in buying or selling.

The island is no place for those who go in the hope of picking up something to do. None but the capitalist, the investor, or the business man with money for his business should go to Porto Rico with anything more in view than an outing or a vacation. As things are at present, there is little enough to interest the capitalist or the investor. The man who is looking for a job should look for it at home; his chances here are infinitely better than they are there. There is absolutely nothing for the position-hunter, for the clerk, or for the workman. In time there may be something, but it will be, at the least, many months before such opportunities are open, and even then they will be few. Until then the case is hopeless, and those who go will but do as their predecessors have done—come home again, poorer and wiser men. If a young man can afford to spend a couple of hundred dollars in the purchase of that particular form of wisdom, the opportunity is open to him there on the island. If he cannot afford it, he will do better not to risk it.

Merchants will find little to do there, except to glean a certain amount of information of rather doubtful accuracy, until the question of tariff rates shall have been definitely settled. There is now nothing on which to base any plans or calculations for business operations. The native merchants are complaining seriously. They are waiting to place orders for hundreds of thousands of dollars' worth of goods, to replenish stocks which have been depleted through many months of uncertain trade conditions, and are losing business which they have been led to expect would be open to them almost immediately after the American occupation of the different cities in which they are located. Nor is it at all easy for an American to obtain any definite information or accurate details regarding any particular line of business and its possibilities. Local commercial methods are not reduced to the system which prevails among American business men. The Porto Rican merchant buys and sells, but I failed to find evidence of that close study of business and business methods by which the American merchant increases his trade and his profits.

Home of the Peons.

It would seem to the American that a few good American stores would be a benefit to the island and a profit to their proprietors. But it is to be remembered that these people have their own ideas, their own tastes, and their own customs, to which ours would be as foreign, and probably as unsatisfactory, as theirs are to us. They may prefer to buy their confectionery in a bar-room. They may prefer haggling over prices instead of being charged a definite and fixed price. They may regard windows in stores and in houses as an abomination. They are the ones most affected by those things, and not we. They are entirely satisfied with a small cup of coffee and a bit of dry bread in the morning, and with a midday lunch, called breakfast, which consists of the same things as the six or seven o'clock dinner, except that breakfast begins with a fried egg, and dinner with a plate of soup.

Dry-goods stores are numerous and the stocks seem fairly good, though often they appear incongruous by their variety. One buys a yard of calico or a saddle, a mantilla or a machete, in the same store. "Who bringeth much brings something unto many," says the prologue in "Faust." That would seem to be the idea of the Porto Rican city merchant. The druggist—and there are many druggists—confines his wares mainly to his particular line. The tailor may or may not carry a line of shirts and hats. A few *zapateria* may sell only shoes, but many of those combinations of dry-goods, hardware, crockery, and saddlery, carry also a line of shoes and slippers. The bakery (*panaderia*) may also sell cigars, cigarettes, and liquors, as may the purveyor of canned goods and delicatessen.

There may be a system to it all, but the stranger cannot tell where he may find the thing he wants. In Ponce I bought a glass of milk, for consumption on the premises, and some cigarettes, at the same place at which I purchased sardines, guava jelly, and fresh eggs. In Yauco I purchased cigars at a store where I might have purchased pencils, ink, and schoolbooks. In a store in Mayaguez I was offered fountain-pens, slippers, straw hats, children's toys, and furniture in the same establishment. If one wishes curios or souvenirs which are distinctive of the island, it is difficult to find them. Few things are manufactured there. Straw hats of local construction are easily obtainable, but one does not care for straw hats for souvenirs. One is offered fans, mantillas, and that sort of things, made in Spain, but the same things can be had in New York at lower prices and in greater variety.

A heavy percentage of the population consists of a class which buys but little. From my observations,

COMMERCE ON THE ISLAND 175

in both city and country, I should say there was little encouragement for dealers in boots and shoes. Men, women, and children, go barefooted. Barefooted they work in the fields. Barefooted they go along the roads and about the towns. Shoes are worn, of course. But neither in Ponce nor in Mayaguez, two of the three largest cities, is there a stock of boots and shoes in any one store which would be considered half a stock in an American city of half their size. In those I have seen there have been few goods of American manufacture.

Much the same remarks are true as regards clothing. The great majority of Porto Ricans do not burden themselves with garments, or with a vast assortment of them. An old hat, a ragged shirt, and a pair of dirty cotton or linen trousers, appear to constitute the entire outfit of most of those whom one meets in going about the country, and of a very noticeable proportion of those seen in the towns. Feminine apparel appears to be equally limited along its special line of construction. There is little to be said about juvenile apparel. Sometimes it consists of a rag; sometimes it does not. Hats are a local industry. The material used is some form of native grass, and a twenty-five cent hat will last a year or two. In house furnishing the same general condition obtains. Dwellings throughout the country are of simple construction and simply furnished.

There are many articles of American manufacture which, if tariff conditions will permit, ought to be successfully introduced into the Porto Rican market. But there would seem to be little chance for American wholesale or retail stores. For the present, at least, little can be done. There must be some definite adjustment of the tariff question. The recognition, or even a tentative recognition, of Porto Rico as a part of the United States, would do much to solve many difficulties. It would give to merchants there a working basis. Commercially, there can be no question that the inclusion of the island as an integral part of the United States would be of mutual advantage. It would give to the people there a broader commercial life, and to us it would give the greater part of what market there is. If to the island is given some form of colonial government, with power to regulate its own customs duties and taxes, its trade with the States on the American continent will be greatly restricted, with no resultant benefit to the people. It would also be placed in a political situation which I am well convinced would be objectionable to the clearest thinking people of the island. They would prefer to be a spoke in the American wheel, rather than a fly upon its rim.

The free opening of the ports of the island to the entry of American goods would give us practically the whole of their trade. Nor would this operate to the disadvantage of the people of the island. We must assume that there will be, in any event, a duty placed on imports from Europe. Free American goods *versus* European goods *plus* a necessary tariff, would economize the cost of living for the majority if not for all. The Porto Rican merchant can now purchase domestics and sheetings, as he does, in Liverpool and Manchester, at a lower figure than he can in New York. An equal tariff on both would exclude the American article. The freedom of the port to the American product would put those goods on the retail market at lower prices than those at which they are now sold. The same applies to other lines which may be regarded as necessaries. The duty on flour has been enormous. Our trade in that article could be very greatly extended and advantage come to both parties. So also with some if not with all forms of paper : Paper bags for grocers and other merchants are a luxury there. They are so costly that they might almost be hung on the walls as ornaments. We can place both flour and paper on the island with profit to ourselves and with advantage to the islanders. We can do many things with beneficial commercial results to ourselves and to them, and the sooner we get the gates open the better it will be for both.

Under wise laws and a just and equitable system of taxation, with a suitable railway system and improved highways, and with the ports of the United States and of the islands open to the exchange of commodities, free of duty, a very material increase of the business of the island will inevitably follow. It is quite possible to double the trade within the next ten or fifteen years. There will be some wild-cat speculation, some unwise investment, and some loss to investors. The schemer and the promoter will find victims who will put their money into companies whose future is wholly hopeless. But along with that there may reasonably be expected a steady growth and improvement. But it will come by gradual increase and development, and not by a sudden bound.

Retail trade and local commerce are in the hands of men who understand it. They know the island people and their requirements. Their ways, ideas, and tastes, are not altogether like ours, but they will, for many years, be better suited for the business of the island. Here and there an American may find a promising opening, and some may find a profitable trade, but, in the main, the American will be handicapped by his ignorance of the needs of the market and the tastes of the people. Porto Rican merchants and Porto Rican people may not be up to our times, but they are up to their own, and they have their own pace in progress. This pace may now be somewhat accelerated, but efforts to force it unduly are not likely to meet with any marked success.

XIII

OLLA PODRIDA

The Best Way to Travel on the Island—Sleeping Accommodations—Conservative Farmers—Food Staples of the Peasantry—The Temperature and Its Results—The Educational Question—Schools and School-houses of San Juan—Points of Interest—Pretty Girls—Cost of City Government—The " Color " Question—Porto Rican Homes.

WOULD anyone go to Porto Rico for a novel experience amid unfamiliar scenes in a strange land? Let him take with him a limited supply of baggage, the less the better, within reasonable limits, but let him carry with him an unlimited supply of determination to put up with whatever he gets. Would any one go for comfort? Let him take with him his own hotel, and his own carriage and horses and driver. To one accustomed to the facilities, the conveniences, and the comforts of the modern American hotel, the Porto Rican affair, in which one eats and sleeps, if sleep he can, offers little beyond an opportunity to be uncomfortable.

The Porto Rican may enjoy his life as keenly as does anyone, but it is after a manner of his own, and that manner would be far from acceptable to the average right-minded American. There should be several moderate-sized fortunes lying around on the island for enterprising American bonifaces who will go there and erect modern hotels on American principles. They need not be palatial. The prime requisite would be that they be provided with windows that will admit light and air. One is led to imagine that the Porto Rican has some bitter feud with both of those rather desirable provisions of nature, so diligently does he seek to exclude them from his buildings, and particularly from his sleeping-rooms.

This applies equally to hotels and to dwelling-houses. I have been in many Porto Rican houses. I have been in the homes of the wealthy, in the dwellings of the middle classes, and in the huts of the indigent. I have seen but few rooms which had anything whatever that would recommend them as sleeping apartments. The salon and the dining-room may be spacious and airy. The bed-chamber will be a den in the most unsuitable corner, small, dark, and cheerless. There may be good reason for this. It is quite probable that the people of Porto Rico are better judges of what is good for them than any stranger could be. The night-air of the island is of doubtful wholesomeness. It may well be that, without stopping too closely to analyze his reasons, the Porto Rican sleeps in what the average American would regard as an air-tight box, for the purpose of avoiding a greater evil. That which to a stranger seems a serious discomfort, becomes an accustomed habit of life, and its discomfort is not noticed as it is by the stranger. To fevers arising from a night-air laden with more or less poisonous exhalations from the rank growth of tropical vegetation one becomes less readily accustomed.

For the exclusion of light there is less apparent reason. It is true that the admission of light means also the admission of some measure of heat. Any increase in temperature is unnecessary, and any means of reducing it is not without its advantages. It is possible also that the cause of the infrequent use of glass runs back to a time when glass was an article of such costliness that its use was practically prohibited. Conservatism is a marked trait of the island people, and the custom of using wooden shutters in the place of windows may be an inheritance from many generations.

This same conservatism manifests itself in many of the habits and customs of the Porto Ricans. Our working oxen are attached to their load so that the strain comes upon the neck and shoulder, where it is supported and backed by the weight of the whole body. In Porto Rico the attachment is made to the base of the horns, the pull coming from the neck and the head, after the manner of the ancient Egyptians. Perhaps from habit, though possibly from other causes, the average Porto Rican farmer ploughs with a pointed stick. The trunk of a small tree of suitable length and diameter forms the beam, which is attached to the yoke at its outer end. At its inner end, adjusted at a proper angle, a strong connection is made with another piece of timber which, by its length and position, serves both as share for cutting and handle for guiding. Some American ploughs are in the market, but thus far they have not found a ready sale. The island methods of cooking are also primitive from an American stand-point, though they are doubtless better adapted to the needs and the conditions of the island than the American contrivances would be.

It is to be remembered that the majority of the islanders are of the peasant class. Their wants are few and simple. Their incomes do not admit any elaborate table supply. Many of them live at a considerable distance from any market, and many articles of table consumption cannot be kept for any length of time in so hot a country. Nor is there necessity for the hearty food which is required by those of a more northern climate. What corn-bread is to the poorer classes of our Southern States, the plantain is to many of the Porto Rican peasantry. It forms the staple diet of many people. It is cooked by boiling, roasting in ashes, or by frying. No American pattern of kitchen-stove is needed for that purpose. The same obtains with rice and beans, both of which figure largely in the Porto Rican bill of fare. In the homes of probably the majority of the people of the island, the American cooking-stove would be only a super-heated nuisance. A goodly number of dwellers in the cities might well find the American kerosene-stove a desirable substitute for the little metal basket of charcoal which is now the usual means of cooking, and the same implement should find some sale through the country.

Aside from any other questions which may affect the menu of Porto Rican households, that of the avoidance of any unnecessary heat is one of no little importance. Nature supplies all the caloric that is really required, and the production of any greater heat than is absolutely necessary for simple forms of cookery is to add unduly to physical discomfort within the house. The climate of Porto Rico is not easily described, though all who write with reference to the island are supposed to say something about it. The weather bureau which has been established by the American authorities since our occupation of the island, will do much to simplify the process of description of climatic conditions. One will now be able to quote statistics from the weather reports instead of attempting to describe his personal sensations.

It is quite safe to start a Porto Rico weather story with the proposition that it is never cold in Porto Rico. A citizen of Ponce, whose English was somewhat limited, said to me, "We never change our clothes in Porto Rico." He did not mean exactly what he said, but he was probably correct in his meaning that the same weight and kind of clothing could be worn the year around with entire comfort. I question if an overcoat could be bought anywhere on the island. So far as I was able to learn there is never a time when even a light top-coat is either necessary or desirable. High up among the hills the thermometer sometimes gets down into the fifties, but even that is unusual. The lowest temperature recorded in San Juan within twenty years, is given by Mr. Hill, in his recently published volume on "Cuba and Porto Rico," as 57.2°.

It is the upper end of the thermometer which has the most work to do. There is more wear and tear on the tube between 75° and 95° than on any other portion of its length. It is not often that the mercury goes above 95°, and that is not reached on many days in the year. Eighty to 90° is the usual run for the summer months, with an average drop of six or seven degrees for the remaining months. The temperature of the island is remarkably equable. The heat, throughout the greater part of the year, is tempered by the ocean breezes from the northeast. During what are our winter months, this wind swings around into the north. But the breeze is constant. Naturally the heat is great in the direct rays of the sun, but the large area of our own Southern States is open to the same criticism. It is always advisable to avoid either work or exposure at midday. That is the practice of the native people. In the larger places many of the stores are closed during the noon hours, and commercial Porto Rico takes advantage of the general quiet to go home to its breakfast.

Nature is really a very kindly old dame, after all. Just as she usually interposes the relief of unconsciousness when a certain measure of pain is reached by a sufferer, so, too, in countries where more than a certain degree of active physical exercise becomes injurious, she interposes a disinclination for exercise. Speaking perhaps more exactly, in hot climates she makes men lazy. That is one of her wise provisions for the benefit of the human race. Along with this disinclination for energetic work, she pours out a lavish bounty which makes energetic work quite needless. It is not so much the excessive heat of Porto Rico that affects one's natural energy. Nor is it that the heat is especially trying, physically. The result is due rather to its continuity and to its character. There are hotter days in New York and in Washington than those which come to Ponce and to San Juan. But, with the exception of occasional brief periods, our northern nights are cooler, and they bring a relief which does not come to the cities of the island. There is also an indescribable difference in the character of the heat. Porto Rican heat saps the energies, both physical and mental. The physical disinclination is accompanied by a mental indifference. It is a beautiful country in which to have a large and airy house with broad, shaded verandas, where one can swing in a hammock and read interesting novels and smoke a pipe, if he has a servant to fill the pipe. Otherwise he will smoke cigarettes, as the natives do, because it is so much less work to light a cigarette than it is to fill a pipe.

For the reading-matter which one might need under such charmingly lazy conditions, it would be quite necessary to depend wholly upon a home supply. The island is not a literary centre. A few insignificant book-shops may be found in some of the larger cities, but the assortment carried is small, and consists mainly of Spanish novels, with a scattering mixture of French productions. A few bulky volumes of statistics and reports are also obtainable, as are sundry volumes of history. San Juan has a small public library. But the Porto Ricans generally are not a reading people. Illiteracy is a well-pronounced epidemic. The census of 1887 gives the following table:

	Male.	Female.	Total.
Able to read and write	57,216	39,651	96,867
Able to read only	5,662	8,851	14,513
Unable to read or write	341,409	353,919	695,328
	404,287	402,421	806,708

This shows, broadly, eighty-six per cent. of the population as wholly illiterate, with twelve per cent. able to read and write and two per cent. able to read only. Such statements as this, however, need a measure of qualification. The 806,708, given as the population, includes all ages from the newly born infant, upward. Some percentage of these, such as those under school-age, should be excepted from estimates, and percentages be based on the remaining number, including only those for whom reading and writing are a possibility. Such a statement could probably be obtained from a complete census report.

The United States authorities give twenty per cent. as the proportion of children of school-age in the entire population. Assuming this figure as sufficiently accurate for general purposes in other lands, we should find 161,340 as the number of Porto Rican children of school age. The public provision for the education of these includes not far from four hundred and fifty school buildings, or about one for each four hundred pupils. But this also needs some qualification. Private schools and private instruction are factors in the general question. There is also the fact of variation in localities. For instance, the city of San Juan is better equipped than some of the rural districts. The same will apply to others of the larger centres. In the fiscal report of San Juan for the year 1897, there are entries of payments made as follows: For one male and one female teacher for the *Escuelas superiores*, the sum of 1,500 pesos each; for one male and one female assistant for the same schools, the sum of 540 pesos each; for six male and six female teachers of the first class for the *Escuelas Municipales*, the sum of 720 pesos each; for one male and one female teacher of the second class, the sum of 540 pesos each.

Assuming the population of San Juan at the present time to be 25,000, which is not far out of the way, and taking twenty per cent. as the relative proportion of children of school age, we find a school-age population of 5,000. For the education of these, payments are made to eighteen teachers, or one teacher for each two hundred and seventy-seven pupils. This estimate, and others of similar character made from the reports of other cities and towns, would indicate that some of the teachers in the country districts are in charge of some very large schools if all the possible scholars of their districts are duly attentive to the opportunities presented for an education. From other entries in the San Juan fiscal report, I infer that each of these eighteen teachers is provided with a separate school building, and I infer also that the buildings are not owned by the city, but are rented from private owners. The terms used are *Asignacion para alquila de casas*, etc., or, practically, "appropriation for renting of houses," etc. The sum paid for the rental of twelve buildings for the municipal schools of the first class, is 4,320 pesos, or 360 pesos for each. The peso is worth from fifty to sixty cents in our money, according to the local rate of exchange. It is wholly evident that there is some room for educational reform on our new island.

Of all the special points of interest on the island, San Juan naturally presents the strongest attractions. Although the small town of Aguada, on the west coast, is perhaps the successful rival of San Juan in point of priority of establishment, the capital city was the more important place even in the year 1511,

Looking Westward from Fort San Cristobal—Morro in the Distance.

Looking Eastward from Morro—San Cristobal in the Distance.

which is the date claimed by both as the time of their founding. San Juan was the head-quarters, if not the home, of Ponce de Leon during the brief time of his governorship of the island. A portion of the government building known as the *Casa Blanca*—the "White House," is shown as the house which that doughty hero occupied during his stay on the island. The massive forts and the extensive fortifications of the city are full of interest for travellers. The Morro and Cristóbal are a mine of wealth for the photographer with an eye for the artistic. But, at the present time, those who enter there leave their cameras behind—with the sentinel at the gateway. Uncle Sam does not approve the photographing of the interiors of his coast defences.

Aside from the fortifications and their immediate surroundings one can see the city of San Juan in a very few minutes. But, like all other places, one may study indefinitely. I am unable to comment upon the life of the city, because of the abnormal conditions which existed at the time of my visit. All was in a state of suspense. The commission was in sitting, preparing the terms and time of the evacuation, and Spanish troops were being assembled for their departure for the Peninsula. The time, in itself, was deeply interesting, but it gave no adequate idea of the real social or commercial life of the place.

More even than is customary, the ladies of the city remained in seclusion.

I have been asked by a number of frivolous young persons of both sexes if I saw any of those delightful creations known as "pretty girls," on the island. I have been obliged to confess that I saw but few such, though I have asserted a very positive conviction that they are to be found there in great numbers. I can at least testify to three in one family of my acquaintance, and can make oath to their powers of delightful entertainment. I have no reason to think that this trio monopolized the beauty of the young ladies of the island, but they surely had enough to give to many who needed it, and still have enough left to warrant any observer in pronouncing them beautiful. I met and saw a few others, but the principal supply of them was concealed by wooden blinds and shutters.

Information, of its particular kind, is found in the fiscal report of the city. The salary of the alcalde is 2,500 pesos per annum. The police force consists of two officers and forty-four guards. The pay of the guards is 360 pesos per annum, a sum equivalent to about two hundred dollars of our money. The city possesses a steam fire-engine for which, fortunately, there is little necessity. The engine is drawn by oxen, and its rush to a conflagration is quite devoid of that thrill of excitement which is caused by the plunging gallop of an American fire-department team. The idea of the oxen probably comes from the fact that there is hardly enough work to do to make it profitable to maintain a stable of large horses, while the little island ponies would never do at all. The municipality is lighted by five hundred electric lights at a cost of thirty-six pesos a year for each light. Street cleaning costs 5,000 pesos per year. The total expenses for the year 1897 are classified as follows:

	Pesos.
City officials	24,417
Police Department	17,485
Fire Department, Lighting, Street Cleaning, etc.	49,260
Public Instruction	27,660
Public Works	6,550
Public Correction	26,351
Interest account, etc.	120,635
City Improvements, including new water-works	249,163
Municipal Charities, including Hospitals, Free Medical Service, etc.	28,962
Special Appropriation	3,000
Total	598,483

Some explanation is needed here regarding the item which occurs in this statement, under the head of Interest Account. That implies a debt, and it was claimed by citizens that neither the island nor its cities carried any bonded indebtedness. A distinction appears to be made between borrowed money and bonded debt. For various publi‧ improvements, such as water-works, etc., the municipality of San Juan has borrowed money from the banks. But the amount is so inconsiderable, and the resources of the city so ample, that comparatively little importance is attached to it. The same may also be true of other cities.

A problem of no little difficulty is presented in the determination of the population of the island along its lines of race and color. The census of 1887 gives the following table:

Blancos (white)	480,267
Pardos (gray)	248,690
Morenos (brown or swarthy)	77,751
Total	806,708

These figures are of somewhat doubtful accuracy. It has been the custom of Spanish officials to misrepresent the relative numbers of whites and blacks in the Spanish colonies and dependencies, and there is some reason for belief that Porto Rico has not been excepted from this custom. It is, however, a fact that Porto Rico is unique among the West Indian islands, in the numerical excess of whites over black in its population. The above list is probably in error in that it includes among the "blancos" a greater or less number whom we in America would regard as "colored," because of some indication of African blood, whether or not that were the source from which the color was derived. Those whites whose whiteness would ever be mistaken for that of the Anglo-Saxon, are not numerous on the island. "White," from the Spanish stand-point, includes many of those of that color with which all are familiar in the faces of some Spaniards, and many West Indians whose veins carry no drop of negro blood. The group indicated as "pardos" includes those whom we should class as "mulattos," while we should probably group the "morenos" with the "blacks." The census list enumerates no "blacks," yet there are such on the island in noticeable numbers. Race lines are drawn to some extent, socially; but race lines, as we know them in America, can hardly be said to exist.

A more hospitable people than our new citizens is not to be found. There is a hesitancy about extending promiscuous invitations to newly made acquaintances to visit them in their homes. But when the invitation does come, it comes heartily, and it is heartily supported by the entertainment which lies behind it. Porto Rican homes may strike the American visitor as bare and inartistic. He may miss

the rugs, the portières, the pictures, and many of
the fanciful trifles to which we are accustomed in
this country. But their absence is due largely to
other reasons than the lack of a developed artistic
taste. Rugs and fabrics of other kinds are encouraging breeding-places for that prolific denizen of all
tropical countries, the *pulex irritans*. There is a coolness in tinted and white walls, and in wooden and
wicker chairs, which is, in such a country, a manifest advantage over the hot stuffiness of upholstery.
If one visits his friends only to see their houses, he
may not be wholly pleased with his visits to Porto
Rican homes. If he goes to meet the people, he will
find them charming, and their home-life delightful.

XIV

THE CAMPAIGN ON THE ISLAND

Military Skill *vs.* the "Dispensations of Providence"—The Plan of the Porto Rico Campaign—A Unique Expedition—General Schwan's Sweep to the West—Difference in American and Spanish Methods in Warfare—Discomforts of a Tropical Campaign—An Unwritten Story—Our Insignificant Casualties.

GENERAL SHAFTER'S argument concerning the Santiago campaign, is the only argument of the whole of the military operations of the Spanish-American engagement of 1898: We won. We forced our opponent to surrender the territory which she had held for centuries. Our navy has commanded the plaudits of the world. Our War Department has merited a sharper criticism and a heavier penalty than is likely to fall upon it. Our military operations, in camp or in field, have brought us little credit excepting that which lies in the fact that we won. Of military skill, of able strategy, of well-conceived and well-executed plan, we have little to boast. The admission is humiliating, but it is the truth. Again and again, I have heard from the lips of officers of our regular army the words, "Surely the Lord has been on our side." Probably this has come from no religious desire to give honor to the "Lord of Hosts." It has come rather as the official testimony of experts that our military victories have been chiefly due to something other than the wisdom and skill of our military leaders. Politics have dominated where military science should have ruled supremé. Incompetent and inexperienced civilians have been appointed to positions which demanded the services of trained and qualified men, and the operations of the line have been obstructed by the blunders and tangles of the staff service.

Out of all this unsavory mass of mismanagement, with its train of unnecessary hardship and sickness, it is pleasant to find even one little incident which cannot be justly criticised. It occurred during the campaign in Porto Rico, and, through a somewhat unusual occurrence, little of public attention has been called to it.

By one of those mysterious dispensations for which it is difficult to account, the only one of the four expeditions which started across the island of Porto Rico, and met with any special degree of success, was unaccompanied by any regular newspaper correspondent. At the time of this movement all of the correspondents then on the island were engaged in watching operations which seemed to be of much

Ruins of Passenger-Cars Burned by the Spaniards at Ponce.

greater importance than that little sweep of a few troops around the western part of the island.

It was a small expedition, composed of regulars and commanded by a regular army officer, Brigadier-General Schwan. General Brooke, General Henry, and General Wilson were in command of the other expeditions, and it was assumed, from the number of their forces and from the routes which they were to follow, that any of these presented opportunities for more interesting and more important news-matter than did that of General Schwan with his little bunch of regulars. That was where an opportunity was lost. As an important and interesting campaign, none of the others even rivalled Schwan's move around the western coast. No one of the others met with such success. No one of them saw so much of active service. No one covered so much territory, or covered so much in so short a time. No one raised the American flag in so many towns and cities.

General Henry was sent across the island, from Ponce, almost due northward to Arecibo. His command was a small one, and it went into a country which had already been opened up by General Stone and the Engineer and Signal Corps, which had entered Adjuntas and Utuado, and was even then on the outskirts of Arecibo, on the northern coast. Some importance seemed to be given to this expedition by rumors that the general-in-chief would follow that route and enter San Juan by the way of Arecibo. General Brooke had landed at Arroyo, and was holding that place and Guayama, and was preparing for his move upon the rear of the Spanish forces which were said to be behind strong entrenchments at Aibonito. General Wilson commanded what was plainly intended to be the main expedition to San Juan until, by his junction with General Brooke at Aibonito, the command of both expeditions, which would then be formed into one army, would devolve upon General Brooke, the ranking officer, and the commanding officer of the corps in which General Wilson commanded a division. There was no doubt that this double expedition constituted the focal point in the campaign, and that Aibonito was regarded as the locality of a decisive battle. It was known that the Spanish troops were there, and that they were making their position into a sort of modern little Thermopylæ.

But the army delayed at Guayama. It was said that they were waiting for supplies which could not be unloaded because of rough water and scarcity of lighters. There were supplies at Ponce and a road of forty miles, bad, but passable under military necessity, from that point to Guayama. It was said that they were waiting for artillery which was on board the Massachusetts, then lying stranded on a reef, while all the available vessels and lighters in the harbor of Ponce were working their hardest to unload her and drag her off before she was pounded to pieces. If artillery was wanted, there were two batteries of the Seventh Regulars, Lemly's and McComb's, in camp at Ponce. They were equipped with the new pattern, smokeless-powder guns, and neither of them fired a shot, and neither was sent where it could fire a shot throughout the campaign.

With the Mayaguez expedition under General Schwan, the case was different. He got ready and started out. The force consisted of about thirteen hundred regulars of the Eleventh Infantry, two batteries of regular artillery, and one troop of regular cavalry. It was to make a general sweep of the west coast and the country behind it, eastward to the route taken by General Henry.

Some of the troops had been landed at Guanica and some at Ponce. A junction was effected at Yauco, and the whole started on its westward trip as an independent expedition. It possessed one or two peculiarities. A brigadier-general commanded what was barely more than a single regiment. It included all three arms of the service, which was wholly correct, though its artillery detachment was entirely out of all proportion to the infantry. A platoon of two guns is all the artillery which is usually supposed to accompany a regiment of infantry, though the point is necessarily elastic and dependent upon general conditions. As a matter of fact, a single platoon was all that did any service on this trip.

The command started in a very business-like way, and appears to have kept up that attitude throughout its course. It was accompanied by its wagon-train, and it kept moving. Beyond Yauco it was the first in the field. In front of it was a force which was its numerical equal, if not its superior. It occupied Sabana Grande and San German practically without opposition. Sabana Grande is the centre of a municipal jurisdiction which includes a population of 9,000 or 10,000. San German is a city of 8,000, with a jurisdiction covering 30,000. About six miles beyond San German, midway between that place and Mayaguez, the troops encountered their first real opposition. At that point, a mile or so to the northward of the main highway, there stands the village of Hormigueros, a small town upon the hill-side. Here an engagement took place. It was short and sharp. The Spanish force had every advantage of position, and had known of the approach of the American force in ample time to give it full opportunity to make its position a strong one. The rolling foothills of the western end of the island's central range, presented all that an army of defence could ask in the way of strategic situation. But the army of Spain stayed not for defences. It fired a few volleys, rose, scattered, and fled like a flock of quail. It had encountered something quite new to its military experience. It did not understand men who followed at a run the bullets they had fired. They did not approve an opponent who fired as he advanced, and advanced as he fired, but always advanced. While it is hardly the correct expression, courtesy suggests that we say that they "retired," they "fell back." They did fall back, and fell over each other in doing so. The Americans followed them.

Mayaguez was occupied practically without resistance, and the army pushed on toward Aguadilla and Lares. Añasco was occupied, and Aguada was virtually occupied. The Spanish troops fell back toward Lares, with the Americans in hot pursuit. They were overtaken on the banks of a river near Las Marias, and a rather snappy little engagement took place. General Schwan's report, I think, gave the Spanish loss as five killed and fourteen wounded. He told me that later reports received from those who came in and from those who were brought in, assured him that the losses from the American firing and from death by drowning in crossing the river, were very many times the number reported. Las

Marias was occupied, and the troops pushed onward toward Lares and toward Aguadilla. Then came the truce. Another twenty-four hours would undoubtedly have found General Schwan in possession of both places, and in control of all the western part of the island. Both places had been practically evacuated. The American losses throughout the whole campaign amounted to two men killed and one officer and seventeen men wounded.

It was not a grand campaign. It was not an affair of which a thrilling history could be written. It occupied barely more than a week. But it was well-planned and well executed, and only came short of complete success through the proclamation of the armistice before it was possible to cover the whole territory. But it was not a picnic. The hospital records will show that. Of the dangers and hardships of such a march it is difficult to obtain an adequate idea without some practical knowledge of the conditions under which it was made. Nor were the troops unduly crowded forward. There was no disregard of life or health. The hardships were only the inevitable attendants of the conditions. If the march was to be made at all, it could only be made as it was made.

To understand what it means to march through drenching rains, and under broiling sun, sleeping at

Commanding Officers of the Twenty-fifth Alphonso Guard, in front of the Spanish Barracks, Arecibo.

night on damp ground and under heavy dews, one needs to try a little of it. I had a very little of it one day, and got all I wanted, when I accompanied a little bunch of the Engineer Corps on a trip across the hills for about eighteen miles. It was not a very bad day either, though we came through a half-dozen mountain showers, which, as I had lost my rain coat the day before, turned me, body and clothing, into a soaked and saturated pulp. I became rather more than a "demned, damp, moist, unpleasant body." Most of the men had their ponchos, but they are a sorry protection against such storms. Then the hot sun would come out and turn everything into a steam-bath with an apparent temperature of several thousand degrees. But I was better off than my companions, for I had a horse to which I could resort if I saw fit, though I was very glad to use him for the benefit of some of the boys, who were limping and hobbling painfully along with blistered feet in worn-out shoes. I saw enough of it, however, to understand fairly well what that sort of thing means.

The merit of the Mayaguez expedition lies in the prompt and business-like way in which it was carried out, in the pluck and the hardihood displayed by the troops who were engaged in it, in the valor shown in such encounters with the enemy as came in their way, and in their patient endurance of hardship and discomfort. Honor lies with these men of our regular army, with the Eleventh Regiment of Infantry, with Troop A of the Fifth Cavalry, with C Battery of the Third and D Battery of the Fifth Artillery. It would also seem fitting that, if there be any stars going as rewards of merit for services during the campaign in Porto Rico, a pair of them be presented to Brigadier-General Schwan, the commander of the expedition in the western part of the island, and thus enable that officer to round out a career of nearly forty years of service in the United States army, from a private in the ranks upward, as a major-general.

The great story of the Porto Rico campaign has not yet been written. It is possible that it may never be written. In view of the outcome of the Porto Rican affair, it is possible that the incident which, in all probability, would have constituted the vital feature of it all, loses its significance and becomes a mere matter of detail, interesting only to military specialists. It would be work for an expert in military science who was well up in the history of war and warfare. This unwritten story might well bear the title, "Would we have been whipped at Aibonito?"

I have alluded to the position as that of a modern Thermopylæ. It perhaps more nearly resembled Plevna, with Spaniards for Turks, and Americans for

Seventh United States Artillery, Light Battery M, Encamped near Ponce.

Russians. When the American officer called upon the Spaniards to surrender upon that somewhat time-worn ground of avoidance of bloodshed, the Spanish leader was not wholly without warrant in replying that if the Americans wished to avoid bloodshed, they would give over their attempt to force the passes to Aibonito and Cayey. Those are not his exact words, but they contain the meaning of his message. As the fight did not come off, we may bluster as we will about what we would have done if it had come off. The opening attack of General Wilson's division on the main road was more of a failure than a success. There are those who were in the line on the Guayama road who do not hesitate to say that had the engagement proceeded instead of being stopped by the arrival of the news of the protocol, the casualties would have been terrible and defeat a probability.

It is probable that the situation was correctly summed up by an officer whose opinion I asked concerning it. He was wholly familiar with the ground, and as he wore a star upon his shoulder-straps, his opinion was not that of a novice. His reply to my question, whether we could have carried the pass, was both concise and comprehensive. "Yes," he said, "we could—in time."

General Schwan's unique little expedition scored

an unqualified success. General Henry's expedition did nothing that would have received six lines in the newspapers during the Civil War. General Wilson's division executed a clever movement on a small scale at Coamo. General Brooke's division did a very small amount of miniature warfare at Guayama. But none of it was real war, as we understand the term from such experiences as the Civil War, the Franco-Prussian, the Russo-Turkish, and the Crimean. In a three weeks' campaign, during which a dozen engagements were reported, our total casualties amounted to three men killed, and four officers and thirty-six men wounded.

Of the discomfort, privations, and sufferings of our troops the story has been fully told in the newspapers. Much of this was wholly unavoidable, though very much might have been prevented or modified by a more efficient staff service, and by the properly systematized organization of such an expedition. But, as General Shafter says of the Santiago campaign, so may we say of the Porto Rican: We won.

XV

UNDER THE OLD RÉGIME

Exaggerated Idea of Spanish Oppression—Heavily Taxed, but Virtually Free from Debt—A Citizen's Complaints—A Nineteenth Century Inquisition—Taxes for Special Purposes—Annexation Preferred to Autonomy—The Hope of the People.

"WHAT everybody believes must be true" is a sweeping proposition. It is too sweeping to be accepted at its full value. One of the things which "everybody believes" is that Spanish domination in Porto Rico, like Spanish rule elsewhere, came little short of being intolerable. Americans have heard much of misrule, oppression, cruelty, and burdensome taxation. We have heard so much of it, and have heard so little in contradiction, that we have come to a general acceptance of almost anything that might be said in condemnation of the Spanish Government in Porto Rico and elsewhere.

It is not my purpose to essay any whitewashing of Spanish colonial government. Its follies and its misdeeds stain too deeply the pages of its history for any apologies or any whitewashing process. But it is possible that we have been misled into an exaggerated idea of the extent of Spain's crimes. Throughout my experience in Porto Rico, I kept in mind this question of Spanish oppression on the island. I heard endless complaints from the island people. But they were, with few exceptions, general and not specific. This led me to some deeper probing. The outcome was the opinion that the Porto Rican has his story of wrongs, real and imaginary; the Spaniard and the Spanish sympathizer have their opinions; and the only thing which appears to be reasonably certain in the matter is that the views of all classes will be magnified, each from its special point.

From the most reliable channels of information which have been open to me—and some of them are quite unimpeachable—I can only conclude that the system of Spanish government in Porto Rico, taken as a system, was admirably constructed. Its laws were adequate and were, in the main, just and equitable. From those who know something of these laws I hear no complaint of the laws themselves. The trouble, then, must be in the abuse of the law by unscrupulous officials. There is one point which is strikingly unique, and for which some credit seems to be due to the Spaniard. Whether it be that the laws make such a thing impossible, or to whatever cause the condition is attributable, I believe that I am correct in saying that Porto Rico, both as a whole, and in the districts and the municipalities which constitute that whole, has no bonded indebtedness. I can learn of none in any part of the island, and the people tell me there is none. Taxes may have been excessive and they may have been unjust, but in view of the absence of city and general bonded indebtedness, it is but just to the Spaniards to admit that they have not "worked the island for all it was worth." Its 3,600 square miles of rich, fertile soil; its populous districts, and its well-to-do little cities and towns, would each and all of them have been capable of carrying a bonded indebtedness whose principal might have gone "where it would do the most good."

But the charges are direct of oppression and of injustice. From talks with many Porto Ricans I am led to the conclusion that it was injustice rather than oppression which galled. Yet I could but smile when talking with one of the most intelligent Porto Ricans of my acquaintance. I was seeking definite charges. "Our courts are corrupt, and our judges are corruptible. Their favorable decision can be, and is, a matter of purchase," he said. I could only remark that this was unfortunate, but neither unique nor original with Porto Rico. "A part of the taxes which we pay only goes to enrich those who impose the tax," he continued. I murmured something about having heard rumors of similar proceedings in my own country. "We have no real voice in our own government. We may have a nominal voice, but we really have no actual voice," was his third charge. I fancy that a somewhat dreamy look crossed my face as I replied that it was quite open to question whether the average American citizen has as much of a voice in his government as he thinks he has. But the fact stands that the people of Porto Rico and the world at large believe that Porto Rico has been misgoverned, and that her governors have enriched themselves at her expense.

I endeavored to obtain a list of the taxes imposed, but was unable to do so, for the reason that so many of them were special taxes and of what may be called local application. The severity of these taxes has restricted trade and commerce, and has, in some cases, impoverished taxpayers through making a continuance of their operations impossible. I am told that, aside from the tariff on merchandise, through the custom-house, there was no system of general taxation applied throughout the island by the insular government. It is possible that the statement may be true. But it is wholly certain that there was collusion and co-operation for mutual benefit between the appointees who imposed the many and diversified local taxes, and the officials of the central government who appointed them. Yet it might be quite as difficult to obtain absolute proof of this, as it would be to account for appropriations made by some state and city governments at home. The evidence is inferential rather than direct. It stands as follows : Vast sums have been collected by taxation; no one can see what has been done with more than a fraction of the collections; officials who came out from Spain either poor or having but little have returned within a brief time possessed of ample means; from three to five years seems to be enough to turn a Lazarus into a Dives, provided Lazarus has a "pull" in Madrid that will send him to Porto Rico in an official capacity.

One of the most burdensome and objectionable taxes imposed was that which was known as the "consumer's tax." It was of local application, and varied somewhat in different localities. It was imposed upon all articles of consumption brought into the city or town for sale. It amounted to a local tariff upon everything which the merchant offered for sale in his store, or which was offered by the little market-gardener from the suburbs, who brought in a basket of eggs or vegetables. Naturally, it very greatly increased the cost of living, while it also tended to a limitation of opportunity for the small farmer.

Another tax was that known as the "domiciliary certificate" (*cedula de vecindad*). It appeared to be a kind of graduated poll-tax, which had nothing to do with the right to vote. It was a certificate of residence and occupation in any given community, and its possession and presentation seem to have been imperative in everything from a horse trade to admission as a pupil in a medical college. Its terms were as follows:

	Pesos per year.
Certificate of the first class	25.00
Certificate of the second class	12.50
Certificate of the third class	6.00
Certificate of the fourth class	5.00
Certificate of the fifth class	2.00
Certificate of the sixth class	1.00
Certificate of the seventh class	.25
Certificate of the eighth class	.10

In the first class were included those whose income amounted to 20,000 pesos per annum, or over. The others were as follows, the figures indicating the income:

	Pesos.
Second class	6,250 to 19,999
Third class	3,250 to 6,249
Fourth class	2,000 to 3,249
Fifth class	750 to 1,999
Sixth class	375 to 749
Seventh class	Less than 375

The eighth class applied to laborers whose work was irregular and whose little income was variable, to men out of employment, etc. I do not understand that the tax was compulsory, but it was represented to me as essential to all men in all walks of life. Beyond these there were special taxes for special purposes, for the war in Cuba, for a hospital for the sick, for roads, railroads, telegraphs, for definite purposes on the island, and for definite purposes on the peninsula. There were fees to be paid for legal documents, civil and criminal, which were invalid unless they bore the official stamp.

All contracts, wills, and documents made before a notary were required to be written on specially stamped paper, costing from fifteen cents to twenty dollars a sheet, according to the position of the maker of the instrument among the twelve different classes. Stamped paper for cases before civil and criminal courts cost from three cents to twenty-five dollars a sheet. Additional sheets, for papers of unusual length, could be had at twenty-five cents the sheet.

But while the long and involved list of taxes stands as a fact, there are ample evidences that all the people of Porto Rico have not been taxed to death. There are thousands of comfortable homes, thousands of men of apparently comfortable incomes.

Nor are these all Spaniards, protected and favored by the officials. There are many well-to-do Porto Ricans. The mass of the people is like the mass elsewhere, in Italy, in Mexico, in China. They are poor, and they are accustomed to poverty. Life is a simple matter in the sunny island, and they are no more discontented than the millions elsewhere.

I quite failed to see wherein the Porto Rican had so much more cause for grumbling than has the average of humanity elsewhere. Beggars were numerous, but there were no signs of suffering poverty. The beggars were largely of the "lame, the halt, and the blind," incapacitated for manual labor.

But these conditions are by no means peculiar to Porto Rico, and there are many places where abject poverty is more apparent, and complaint less vigorous. Complaint of something is universal. We of the United States do our full share of it. We complain of our taxes, our laws, and our administration. The protectionist and the free-trader alike complain of the tariff. The workingman complains of the greed of the capitalist, and the capitalist complains of the unreasonable demands of the workingman. The Porto Ricans have made the most that they could out of the fact that they have been subjects ruled by an outside power, and have been given little or no voice in the regulation of their own affairs. Of this and of one other thing they complain more bitterly than they do about their taxes. They charge the government with marked partiality toward Spanish residents. Taxation was unequal, and when opposed to the Spaniard before the courts the Porto Ricans found no justice. These constitute the complaints of the more intelligent, as I have met them. They are the demand of men for fair-play, self-government, and individuality.

According to statements made to me by one of the leading men of the Autonomist party in Porto Rico, that party is far better satisfied to have the island come under American control than it would have been with any form of autonomy or independence. Autonomy was regarded as greatly preferable to Spanish rule and robbery, when there was no thought or hope for American occupation. The argument used is that, as a part of the United States, the island will share the progress, the development, and the freedom of that country, whose moral and physical support it will now have in all its relations with other countries. As an independent government it would become as Venezuela, Hayti, San Domingo, *et al.*, torn with domestic dissension and frequent political revolutions.

The prevailing belief is that Porto Rico will be developed, and that Porto Ricans will be enriched, by the advent of American people and American capital. The people have heard of American wealth and energy, of our development and enrichment of all that we touch, and they look for personal advantages to arise from our control of their island. They are not a naturally energetic people. The tropical sun acts, as usual, as a negative force in the matter of active industry. But they appear to recognize certain possibilities of which their island is capable, and to have, at least, a theoretical idea of their development. In spite of all talk of Spanish robbery and oppression, of heavy taxes and financial imposition, there are wealthy men on the island of Porto Rico. The majority are poor, as the majority are almost universally. There is no doubt that there is little opportunity for the poor man. He can make what passes for a living—that is, he can live and his family can live. But land is dear, and the island appears to be a place for capital to develop in ways that will enrich the investor and give to its employees a better opportunity for a better living.

XVI

ADIOS! ESPAÑA

A Brief but Impressive Ceremony—The De Profundis of Spanish Rule—Amicable Relations—Admiral Sampson's System of Ventilation for Public Buildings—The Fortifications of San Juan—The Soldiers of the Boy King—Their Repatriation—The Law of Karma.

THE Governor's Palace in San Juan stands across the western end of Fortaleza Street. It is a large and somewhat imposing structure, though of no impressive style of architecture. In the shade of an angle formed by the junction of a wing with the main building, there stood, a little before twelve o'clock at noon, on October 18th, some two score officers of the American army and navy. They were all in so much of dress uniform as their campaign outfit permitted, and wore their side arms. With them were six or eight civilians, some in dress and some in frock coats. These were foreign consuls, and members of the insular government of the island of Porto Rico.

Immediately in front of this group, and facing the arched portal of the Palace, stood the regimental band of the Eleventh United States Infantry. Behind the band, filling the street from curb to curb, stood two battalions of the Eleventh. Their uniform consisted of campaign hats, blue flannel shirts, trousers of the kind furnished to the troops for the campaign in the tropics, and the brown regulation leggings. They presented no brilliant spectacle, those tall, sunburned soldier-men, but the Spaniards in the western part of the island ran away from them a few weeks before. Behind the infantry, Troop H of the Sixth United States Cavalry sat on their big bay horses, with drawn sabres. They presented no more gorgeous appearance than did their fellows who stood in front of them, but the Sixth Cavalry, or any part of it, is the Sixth.

On the balcony of the first story of the Palace stood a little group of ladies and gentlemen. Among them was Mrs. Gordon, whose husband stood with his associates, Admiral Schley, and General Brooke, of the United States Commission, among the group of officials. Outside the military lines and up the adjacent streets, on roofs and balconies, and at the windows of the Palace and other buildings of the vicinity, were soldiers and civilians, ladies and children.

Just before the stroke of noon all movement ceases, all voices are still. The heads of all officials are bared, as are the heads of all spectators who are blessed with any sense of the fitness of things. There is an instant of impressive silence. To all save the shallow and the thoughtless the moment is one of deep solemnity. Many eyes are wet, and many a lip quivers with intensity of feeling. Into the grave of the past there fall four centuries of history of Spanish power in sea-girt Porto Rico. It is the end of a long life, mis-spent if you will, but venerable in its antiquity if in nothing else. Then upon the hushed air there sounds the musical note of a distant bell slowly striking the hour. Upon its third stroke a second bell chimes in, and then a third. While they are still sounding, there comes the roar of the signal-gun, fired by Major Day of the Fifth United States Artillery, from the walls of the old Morro. Before the sound of the gun has died away, the band strikes up the sweet strains of our national anthem, as the Stars and Stripes are slowly hauled to the masthead on the top of the Palace by Major Dean and Lieutenant Castle of General Brooke's personal staff. With the dying notes of "The Star-Spangled Banner" the spectators give three hearty cheers, the inevitable, enthusiast howls "tiger-r-r-r," and the ceremony is over. The troops march away to their barracks; carriages drive up to take the officials to their homes or to the hotels, and the little crowd of spectators melts away in different directions.

It was all a quiet affair. There was no excitement, and but little enthusiasm. An hour after its close the streets had assumed their wonted appearance. There was little to show that anything important had taken place, that by this brief ceremony Spain's power on the island of Porto Rico had ended forever. There was little to indicate a change, except that over the grim walls of the Morro, over the frowning heights of San Cristóbal, and over all the public buildings of the city, there shone the bright colors of the red, white, and blue, instead of the red and yellow of Spain.

There was a deal of handshaking among the two or three hundred American civilians gathered in the city. A cork or two popped, and a few less effervescent and more economical throat-moisteners went down to an accompaniment of, "Well! Here's to——" whatever it might be. Blue flannel shirts and campaign hats took the place of linen blouses and white helmets on the streets, as the Krag-Jorgensen was substituted for the Mauser and the old-pattern Remington. Here and there a native showed the new national colors, and a few householders and merchants displayed the American flag. But the event had been anticipated. Flag-raising in Porto

Fort San Cristobal, San Juan.

Rico had got to be an old story. The citizens of San Juan had already become quite familiar with the appearance of American soldiers and civilians on their streets, and the proportion of ardent supporters of the new government was not of sufficient strength to lead to any very effusive demonstrations on the part of citizens.

Under the circumstances, all was best as it was. It was far better than any great parade of armed troops. It was better that there were no long speeches and ceremonial forms. We have hardly laid a big enough egg to warrant our doing any great amount of cackling. All was done that was necessary. The national salute of twenty-one guns was fired from the different forts, and the American ships in the harbor were dressed from stem to topmast, and from topmast to stern, with all their bunting. The revenue-cutter Manning was the only government vessel there, except two or three transports. She echoed the cannon from the forts with the proper twenty-one shots from her guns.

None of the Spanish Commission was present at the ceremonies at the palace. Some had gone to Spain, and the one who was still there did not attend. By a special invitation extended by the United States Commission, all the chiefs of the insular government were among the guests of the occasion, as were also the different foreign consuls. The people of the city were happily disappointed in their apprehensions of disturbance on the part of the anti-Spanish element, and the order which garrisoned the city with the Eleventh Regulars eliminated much of the danger of rowdyism on the part of our soldiers.

The war in Porto Rico is over. It ends with much of hopeful outlook for the future. Much will depend on the judgment, the tact, and the breadth of view of our officials. There are a few small clouds in the morning sky, but they will be easily dissipated, and the coming years should be a time of sure and steady growth and development for this spot for which a beneficent Creator has done so much.

The days which preceded this simple but impressive ceremony presented a peculiarly interesting study for the observer of unusual situations. It was the twilight of Spanish domination in the island. One might easily grow sentimental over it, for, cruel and unjust as may have been the Spanish rule on the island, there was a pathos in its downfall. It was the end of an old life and the beginning of a new.

A different condition was presented in the old city of San Juan from that which obtained in Ponce, in Mayaguez, and elsewhere. In those places the American occupation was an affair of some abruptness. It had not been immediately anticipated by the people, and the appearance of a large body of fighting men was followed by the hasty and precipitate departure of the Spanish garrisons. There was another point of essential difference. In the territory first occupied by the Americans the native Porto Rican element, with its strongly indicated disposition to welcome the change in its rulers, was very greatly in excess of the Spanish population and that class which is counted as of Spanish sympathies. In San Juan the condition was reversed. The Spanish element there outnumbers the Porto Rican by about three to one.

From such a situation it might reasonably be inferred that, prior to the arrival of the American army, there would be some such manifestations as those which appeared in some of our Southern cities just before the outbreak of the Civil War, in Paris upon the declaration of war with Germany, and elsewhere under similar conditions. But I saw nothing of the sort. Here and there one got an ungracious look; here and there a merchant was neither very alert nor very courteous in attending to the wants of an American customer. But of an open, overt act of any kind which could reasonably be construed into an intended insult, or which clearly displayed any bitter animosity, I saw no sign, nor did I hear of any. There in what it would hardly be an exaggeration to class as a Spanish hot-bed, dominated by Spaniards and Spanish sympathizers, and filled with the soldiers of the Spanish army, there was a little handful of Americans. Encamped some fifteen miles or so outside of the city, to the southeast, was the troop of United States cavalry which served as an escort to Major-General Brooke, United States commissioner and general in command of all the American forces on the island. A score or more of American civilians, journalists, and merchants investigating commercial questions, were quartered in the two leading hotels. Or, rather, they were quartered in the leading hotel, the Inglaterra, and another, the Francia, which bears to the Inglaterra about the same relation that the old Metropolitan Hotel in New York would bear, were it still standing, to the Waldorf-Astoria.

The rest of the American contingent was represented by the commission and its staff. It was only a small group among so many who could hardly be expected to regard the people of America with the most kindly of feelings. But until all possible danger had passed, down there in the harbor, within a few hundred yards of any part of the little island upon which stands the city proper of San Juan, there lay a little bunch of graceful, but grim-looking, slate-colored vessels showing the bright folds of the

Plaza in San Juan, with the City Hall on the Left.

American flag. The fact that these could have materially altered the architectural lines of the city in the course of a short hour or two, may have had some influence as a restraining element. But it is more probable that the absence of any aggressive or protesting demonstration arose from a general acceptance of the situation, and a realization of the uselessness of any disturbance.

All was quiet and peaceful. But wait—I am in error. San Juan can never be regarded as "quiet" so long as it tolerates the cries of street venders who, in the continuity of their howling and its harshness, turn the strains of the New York representative of the same fraternity into the occasional warblings of angel bands. But peaceful it certainly was in San Juan. There was but little business being done. There was none of that long procession of bullock-teams and army-wagons, none of that hurrying of carriages to and fro, which was a noticeable feature of the city of Ponce. The only busy places in San Juan were the cafés. The Mallorquina is the best and most fashionable of these, and during a part of the day, and a considerable part of the night, it and its rivals were thronged by a somewhat curious mixture of Spanish and American uniforms, military and naval, with Spanish and Porto Rican and American civilians all hobnobbing sociably together, elbow to elbow, over ices and glasses of mild and cooling drinks. There was little drunkenness, and such as there was, I regret to say, was American.

Conflicting reports have gone out with reference to the extent of the damage done to the city by Admiral Sampson during his brief use of the place as a target for his guns. It is a fact that the city generally shows but little sign of having been used as an object for target-practice. Here and there some of the taller buildings show scratches and minor gaps made in their superstructure by low-flying shells which were intended to pass over the city, and drop upon any possible Spanish squadron which might be hidden in the inner bay. But in the walls of some of the military buildings immediately upon the northern shore, and in the walls of some of the structures in their vicinity, one sees a number of holes, which are evidently the result of a definite purpose to make holes in them. It may be that little damage was done. I can only say that I have no wish to have any buildings which may come into my possession at any time ventilated by the system employed by Admiral Sampson upon some of these Spanish barracks and fortifications.

There is little question that the deliberate and sustained bombardment of San Juan by an American squadron, having the demolition of the city as its intent and purpose, would have very speedily reduced the major portion of it to dust and ashes. That it was not done is due solely to the fact that it was never attempted. Enough was done to necessitate the use of a considerable quantity of bricks and mortar in repairing damages, and, at the time of the Sampson episode, to drive the majority of the people of the city, many of them clad only in the scantiest of habiliments, and some of them robed only in sheets, in the dim light of the early morning, to seek refuge and shelter in the mountains of Bayamon.

But now that the disturbance is all over, and we have had opportunity for competent official examination of the fortifications of the city, it will be no more than common honesty for us to acknowledge that we must have pounded away at those massive walls for an indefinite time before we could have compelled them to haul down their flag. This fact makes for our own advantage if it ever becomes necessary for us to defend our new possession. Equipped with modern guns aimed by American gunners, the forts of San Juan could be made extremely offensive and dangerous to an attacking fleet. It is even quite probable that in a sustained bombardment the American fleet would not have come off scathless from the Spanish defence. A few well-aimed shots, or even a few chance shots, from Morro, from San Cristóbal, or from the eastward extending fortification, might easily have cost us a vessel or two and a few hundred lives. Had San Juan been defended, as it might readily have been, against attack by land or sea, the story of the Porto Rican campaign would have been one of tragedy rather than semi-comedy.

We had little opportunity to note the fighting quality of the Spanish soldiers in Porto Rico. We had no real battles with them. But in one department of their military life, these men commanded the respect of all who observed their conduct. During the three weeks preceding their embarkation for the Peninsula, I saw upward of 5,000 Spanish soldiers. The streets of the city of San Juan were full of them at all hours of the day. Within that time they received, not only the arrears of their pay, but two months' pay in advance as well. They had money and there is an ample supply of cafés and saloons in the city. I have yet to see an intoxicated Spanish soldier. A friend tells me that he saw two whom he describes as being "just gentlemanly drunk." Quiet, orderly, respectful in demeanor, though not remarkably soldierly in their bearing, the troops of the boy king have received the highest praise for their conduct from all with whom I have discussed them.

St. John's Church, San Juan, showing the Effects of the Bombardment.

Among the soldiers who turned their faces to the land of their homes and of their own people, were those who cast many a backward look and who felt and expressed their keen regret that they must go. Some regretted the conditions under which they went, for, gloss it as they might with talk of the preservation of honor, they went defeated, and they went not because they would, but because they must. Some will return. There are those who, charmed by all that nature has done to make the island so rich and so attractive, announced their purpose to come back and make their homes there, even though it meant the spending of their lives under the flag of those who had been their opponents, and apparently their enemies. They had established ties of friendship during their stay. Not a few were bound by even closer ties. Some had married women of the island, and their children are Porto Ricans. Some were glad to go. Many seemed to be wholly indifferent. Orders sent them there, and orders sent them back again. It was not their affair, and the future government of Porto Rico, whether it be Spaniard or by Yankee, was nothing to them.

I had fancied that the process of embarkation would be attended by many evidences of emotion, of joy or sorrow, of pleasure or regret. There was little display of feeling. The transports which were to take those who were to go by the expedition of October 3d and 4th, lay at anchor a hundred yards or so from the sea-wall. In squads and in companies the troops marched to the water-front and waited their turn to be packed on the lighters upon which they were ferried across to the ships. Here and there a hat was waved and a voice called a farewell message. There was little enthusiasm of any kind, little show of interest. The quiet was not the subdued quiet of sadness, but rather that of general indifference. There were spectators, but no crowd.

The Isla de Panay and the Satrustegui, the ships provided for this detachment, were fine, large vessels from Barcelona. The Panay is said to have taken 1,600 soldiers and some civilians, while the Satrustegui is reported as having carried 2,300. Whether these figures be accurate or not, there is no question that they were packed about as solidly as a box of figs. As the vessels lay in the harbor, their decks presented a dense mass of human forms moving about in a slow but restless entanglement, with a bordering fringe of other figures which hung along and over the rail upon both sides of the ships. Many of the transports which have taken our own troops to ports in the Antilles have been thought to be well packed with passengers, and there has been some complaint because of it. Some of the dissatisfied might have learned a lesson or two in troop transportation had they been assigned a passage on board these Spanish vessels. It would have been of more interest than pleasure to make the trip with these returning troops, for the purpose of noting the accommodations, and the quantity and quality of the food supplied to them. I have my doubts about a *menu* which included the canned beef and the salmon, the beans and tomatoes, which some of those who went out there on the Mohawk, the D. H. Miller, and the Massachusetts found so unpalatable.

The evacuation of the city of San Juan, the Spanish stronghold upon the island, the focal point of Spanish people and Spanish influence, was the closing of the gate of an old homestead which has seen generation after generation come and go for four hundred years. The mortgage upon the broad and fertile acres has been foreclosed by the operation of that inexorable law which says : "That which a man soweth, that shall he also reap." The property passes into the hands of others who, it is much to be hoped, will deal wisely and honestly with it.

INDEX

ADJUNTAS, 65, 68, 79, 80, 199; the population, 67; the approach to, 69-71; location, 72; the city hall, 73; the police force, 74; the parish priest, 74-76; the sale of liquor, 76; natural surroundings, 77
Agricultural implements, 169
Agricultural products:
  Coffee, 72, 95, 106, 124, 132-133, 151, 153-155, 170
  Corn, 94-95, 160, 171
  Sugar, 106, 117, 131, 142, 151-153, 156, 170
  Tobacco, 44, 151, 156-158, 170. See Cigars
  Vegetables and fruits, 64, 159-160, 170. See Fruits
Aguada, 136, 190, 203
Aguadilla, 104, 122, 136, 203, 204
Aibonito, 114-115, 200, 206, 207
Añasco, 136, 203
Arecibo, 68, 79, 122, 136, 199, 200
Arroyo, 117, 200

BAY RUM, 171
Bayamon, 136, 229
Beans, 184
Beef, amount of, imported, 170
Books, 187
Boots and shoes, the trade in, 170, 174, 175
Boriquén, 26, 27, 29, 104

Brooke, General, 6, 10, 199, 208, 220, 221, 226
Butter, 170

CABLES, 148-149
Caguas, 118, 144
Camuy, 136
Candles, 170
Carolina, 136
Casino, the, at Mayaguez, 105
Cattle-raising, 160, 171
Cayey, 115, 116, 144, 207
Cheese, 170
Chinaware, 170
Church architecture, 117
Cigars, 44, 77, 156-158
Clothing, 175
Coal, 170
Coamo, 110, 113, 208; the baths of, 111
Cocoa-nuts, 63, 131, 158
Coffee, the crops and the industry, 72, 95, 151; amount exported, 106, 170; annual output of the island, 124, 153; expenses of transportation, 124; possibilities of the industry, 132-133, 155; the chief district, 154; coffee raising profitable, 154-155, but labor and time involved, 155-156
Commerce, effect of tariff rates on the problem of, 165; prospects of, 166 *et seq.;* business methods in Porto Rico, 172 *et seq.;* the

commercial advantage of annexation, 176–179. See Industries.
Cooking, 184
Copper, 150
Corn, 94–95, 160, 171
Coto Laurel, 109
Cotton goods, 169
Cristóbal. See San Cristóbal.
Cuba, 4, 21; tobacco exported to, 157

DAIQUIRI, 24
Dress, the, of Porto Ricans, 39, 175
Dry-goods, 173. See Shops.

ERNST, GENERAL, 6, 10, 113, 114
Exports:
 Cattle, 171
 Coffee, 72, 106, 153, 157, 179
 Corn, 171
 Fruits and vegetables, 158–159, 171
 Guano, 171
 Hides, 171
 Lumber, 171
 Molasses, 170
 Rum, 171
 Sugar, 106, 151–153, 179
 Tobacco, 156–158, 170
 See also Commerce, Industries

FAJARDO, 25, 122
Fish, 169
Flour, 44, 169, 177
Français, Hotel, 48, 50, 166
Fruits, 64, 131; obstacles to the export fruit-trade, 158; amount exported, 171. See Cocoa-nuts, Mangoes, Oranges

GALENA, 150
Glassware, 170

Gold, 150
Grape fruit, 158
Guanica, 25, 63, 66, 125, 201; situation of, 62, 67
Guano, 171
Guayama, 200; the road to, 116; the church, 117; a transportation centre, 122; General Brooke at, 208
Guayanilla, 136, 140

HATS, 174–175
Henry, General, 66, 68, 79, 80; the expedition of, 199–201, 208
Hides, 171
Highways, 122 *et seq.*; the road from Ponce to San Juan, 108–121; repairs, 119; new roads needed, 120–121; military roads, 123; roads required to assist in American development of the island, 124–125, 178; driving through mud, 126–128; Porto Ricans bad drivers, 129–130; adverse conditions in the soil, 131–132; mountain highways, 132; a suggested method of developing Porto Rico, 133–134; effect of a new highway system on sugar-raising, 153
Hormigueros, 93, 98, 136; Captain Hoyt at, 99; the church of Our Lady of Monserrate, 100; the battle at, 202–203
Hotels, 180–181
Houses, 70, 73, 101, 102; furnishings of, 176; bed-chambers, 181–182; hospitality *versus* furniture, 195–196
Humacao, 122

ICE, 44
Illiteracy, 187–190

INDEX

Imports, 166; annual value of various imports estimated, 168-170
Industries:
  Cattle-raising, 160, 171
  Coffee-growing, 72, 95, 124, 132-133, 151, 153-156
  Fruit-raising, 131, 158-159
  Lumbering, 151
  Mechanical industries; 160
  Mining, 150-151
  Sugar-raising, 131; in Guayama, 117; handicapped by cost of transportation, 142; possibilities of, 151-153; small plantations, 156
  Tobacco-growing, 151, 156-158
  Vegetable-gardening, 64, 159-160, 170
  See Agricultural Products, Manufactures, and Commerce
Iron, 150
Isla de Panay, 232

JOHNSTON, CAPTAIN, the expedition of, 80 *et seq.*
Juana Diaz, 110

LA PLAYA. See Playa, La
Labor, inefficiency of, 146; little encouragement in the situation, 171-172
Land, the cost of, 145, 160
Lares, 80, 144, 203, 204
Las Marias, 203, 204
Lee, General Fitzhugh, 1, 2, 5
Leon, Ponce de, 191
Liquors, sale of, 77; amount of, imported, 170. See Rum
Lumber, 146, 151, 170, 171

MANGOES, 39, 40, 41, 64, 158
Manufactures:
  Cigars, 44, 77, 156-158

Hats, 174, 175
Ice, 44
Molasses, 151, 170
Rum, 77, 119-120, 151, 171
Marketing, Sunday, 63-65
Mayaguez, 56, 93, 122, 136, 137, 144, 174, 175, 202, 205, 224; houses, 101; streets and street cars, 102-103; the Columbus monument, 104; the Casino, 105; the harbor, 106; exports, 106; its attractiveness, 107; from Yauco to Mayaguez, 125 *et seq.*; the Mayaguez expedition of General Schwan, 201-208; Mayaguez occupied by American soldiers, 203
Mechanical industries, 160
Miles, General, 7, 10, 25, 29, 112
Miller, the D. H., 9, 31, 233; voyage of the, 11-25
Millon, Padre Antonio, 74
Mining, 150-151
Mohawk, the, 13, 233
Molasses, 151, 170
Morro, the, 191, 221, 222, 230

NEGROES, 194-195

ORANGES, 64, 158-159

PAPER, 177
Pedlers, 40, 163
Peso, value of the, 190
Pine-apples, 64, 158
Pines, the Isle of, 21
Plantain, 184
Playa, La, 34, 35, 52; activity in, 48-50
Ploughing, 183
Ponce, 25, 32, 65, 76, 78, 79, 93, 107, 122, 125, 199, 200, 201, 224, 227; natural surroundings, 30-31; the

238 INDEX

port city of La Playa, 34, 35; the city proper, 36; the park, and the cathedral, 37; activity along the Ponce road, 38; the people, 39, 40; shops, 42-44, 57-58, 174-175; the crowd at La Playa, 48-49; the Hôtel Français, 50; Ponce from the stranger's point of view, 52; the theatre of La Perla, the casino, and the promenade on the plaza, 53; the police department, 54; the fire department, 55; the market, 56; the road to San Juan, 108; the Ponce and Yauco railroad, 136; the railway station at Ponce, 137; by rail to Yauco, 139 *et seq.;* the cost of a drive to San Juan, 143

Ponce, the San Juan road from, the great excellence of, 108-109; Juana Diaz and Coamo, 110-111; exposed as a military road, 112; scenery, 113; Aibonito and Cayey, 114-115; trees, 116; Guayama, and sugar-raising, 117, Rio Piedras, 118; repairing the road, 119; the need of new highways, 120-121; cost of travel over, 143

Ponies, 34, 41-42, 71, 102, 125-126; better horses needed in Porto Rico, 130

Pork, 160, 169

Porto Rico, 1, 2, 3, *et passim;* the departure of the Porto Rican expedition, 1-10; the Carib name of the island, 26-27; the Spanish name, 28-29; first impressions of the island, 30 *et seq.;* area, 123, 167, 211; number of miles of highway, 123; character of the soil, 131-132; relative area of the mountain district, 133; railroads, 135 *et seq.;* belt and cross country lines, 144 *et seq.;* industrial possibilities, 150 *et seq.;* an "American Bermuda," 159; commerce, 163 *et seq.;* density of the population, 167; advantages of annexation to the United States, 176-179, 217-218; the peasant population, 183; climate, 184-187; illiteracy, 187-190; proportion of the white to the dark population, 194-195; Porto Rican hospitality, 195-196; ideas of Spanish oppression exaggerated, 209 *et seq.;* good government, 210; freedom from debt, 211; taxation, 212 *et seq.;* poverty and wealth, 215, 216; the sacrifice of Spanish power, 219 *et seq.*

RAILWAYS, lack of, 123; number of miles operated, 135-136; routes, 136; the railway station at Ponce, 137; by rail from Ponce to Yauco, 139 *et seq.;* a railway system needed in Porto Rico, 142, 153, 178; the belt line, 135, 142, 144; a cross-country line desirable, 144; the expense of construction, 145 *et seq.;* ownership of the present system, 146-147

Rice, 169, 184

Rincón, 136

Rio Piedras, 118, 136, 137

Road houses, 119

Roads. See Highways

Rum, Porto Rican, 77, 119, 120, 151, 171

SABANA GRANDE, 93, 126; houses, 94; corn and coffee, 95; population of, 202

INDEX 239

Samana Bay, 24, 25
San Cristóbal, 191, 222, 230
San German, 93; picturesqueness of, 95; "Hotel the Struggle," 96-97; population, 202
San Juan, 2, 28, 79, 107, 111, 113, 122, 136, 143, 200, 233; the monument to Columbus, 104; the road to Ponce, 108; the expense of a drive to Ponce, 143; antiquity of San Juan, 168; schools, 189-190; attractions of the city, 190-191; fortifications, 191, 229; expenses of the municipal government, 192 et seq.; the ox-cart fire-engine, 192; the Governor's Palace, 219; an impressive ceremony, 219 et seq.; the large Spanish element, 224-225; a quiet city, 227; the Mallorquina, 227; the damage done by Admiral Sampson's fleet, 228; Spanish soldiers in San Juan, 230 et seq.
San Juan road, the, from Ponce, 108; excellence of, as a bicycle path, 109; Juana Diaz and Coamo, 110-111; exposed as a military road, 112; scenery, 113; Aibonito and Cayey, 114-115; trees, 116; Guayama and sugar-raising, 117; Rio Piedras, 118; repairing the road, 119; new highways needed, 120-121; driving from San Juan to Ponce, 143
San Juan Bautista, 28, 29
Santiago, 8, 9, 10, 25, 32
Santiago expedition, the, 4, 7
Satrustegui, the, 232
Schools, 188-190
Schwan, Brigadier-General, the campaign of, 199, 201-208
"Shacks," 94

Shafter, General, 197, 208
Shoes, 170, 174, 175
Shops, 43 et seq., 57 et seq., 76, 94, 173 et seq.
Smoking, enjoyed by women, 77
Spain, products of, in Porto Rico, 43, 170, 174; sacrifice of the power of, in Porto Rico, 219 et seq.
Spanish, the traveller's vocabulary of, 59-61
Stone, General Roy, 68, 199
Street-cars, 102-103
Street-lights, 193
Sugar raising, extent of, and amount of the product exported, 106, 170; in the vicinity of Guayama, 117; the black soil both the bane and the blessing of the planter, 131; the lowlands the best sugar lands, 132; effect of railway improvements on the industry, 142, 153; possibilities of, 151 et seq.; amount of capital required, 152; small plantations, 156

TALLABOA, 136, 140
Tariff, 165, 172, 176, 177
Taxes, 120-121, 212-215
Telegraphs, the present system of, 147 et seq.; under American control, 148; cable lines, 148-149
Timber. See Lumber
Tobacco, 151; possibilities of tobacco raising, 156 et seq.; Porto Rican cigars, 44, 77, 157-158, 174; amount of, exported, 170
Toro, Captain Miguel, 95
Transportation, 120, 122; common modes of, 123; roads needed, 124-125; railways needed to develop sugar-raising and other in-

dustries, 142, 153; transportation by water, 143; the best way to travel, 180. See also Highways, Railways

Trees, 116

UTUADO, 75, 76, 79, 199

VEGETABLE-GARDENING, 64, 159-160, 170

Villas, 70. See also Houses

WILSON, GENERAL, 199, 200, 207, 208

Woollen goods, 169

YAUCO, 93, 174, 201, 202; location, 62; the plaza, 63; Sunday marketing, 63-65; the Guanica road, 66; Hotel Victoria, 125; the road to Mayaguez, 126; the Ponce and Yauco railroad, 136 *et seq.*

er the Spanish administration, was open.

· —), and boundaries of the departments (······).

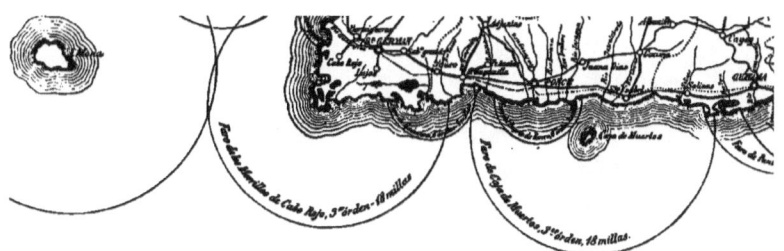

PORTO RICO AND ITS COAST LINE.

Showing the light-houses (●), cities (◉), towns (○), military roads (———), country roads (- - -), railways (······), railways in process of construction (— · —

BOOKS ON OUR NEW POSSESSIONS

COMMERCIAL CUBA

A Book for Business Men

By WILLIAM J. CLARK

With 8 maps, 7 plans of cities, and 40 full-page illustrations, and a Commercial Directory of Cuba. Large 8vo, $4.00

"A THOROUGHLY good and useful book. We should not know where to find within another pair of covers so much and so carefully sifted information bearing on this subject. Mr. Clark's painstaking account of the railway and telegraph systems; of highways and harbors; of rivers and water supplies, and lighthouses; of sugar and tobacco growing; and his detailed description of each province and of every city of any size, together with a 'business directory' for the whole island, make his book one of great value for reference as well as for practical guidance. In the present situation of Cuban affairs it should command a wide sale. Its accuracy is certainly of a high order."—New York *Evening Post.*

YESTERDAYS IN THE PHILIPPINES

By JOSEPH EARLE STEVENS

With 32 full-page illustrations from photographs by the author. *Seventh thousand.* 12mo, $1.50

"WITH the observant and indulgent eye of an old traveller, Mr. Stevens has seen everything in the islands worth seeing, and has described what he has seen in a most interesting manner. . . . All is set forth by the narrator in a breezy, chatty way that would be entertaining under any circumstances."
—Philadelphia *Evening Telegraph.*

CHARLES SCRIBNER'S SONS, NEW YORK

THE WAR ON SEA AND LAND

THE CUBAN AND PORTO RICAN CAMPAIGNS

By RICHARD HARDING DAVIS

With 117 illustrations from photographs and with 4 maps. *Twentieth thousand.* 12mo, $1.50

"NEVER has a war been reported as this has been, and never has a history been written like this, by one who saw it all—while the blood was hot and the memory vivid."—New York *World*.

"THIS is much the most vivid and readable of all the books on the war that have appeared so far, and it is full of life and color and incidents that show the sort of stuff of which our soldiers were made. The book is written with a keenness, a vivacity, a skill and a power to thrill and to leave an impression which mark a decided advance over anything that even Mr. Davis has written heretofore."—Boston *Herald*.

OUR NAVY IN THE WAR WITH SPAIN

By JOHN R. SPEARS

Author of "The History of Our Navy"

With 125 illustrations from photographs and with charts and diagrams. 12mo, $2.00

"MR. SPEARS has plainly put his best efforts into that mighty combat, the sea-Gettysburg of the war, the death-grapple of Cervera's ships and Sampson's. His story of the action of July 3d is superb. It is the most lucid and comprehensive description which has yet been laid before the American people, and it is made all the more valuable by the official chart of the ships' courses which accompanies it. As a whole, Mr. Spears's book is not only true to technical details, but it is a spirited and admirable piece of literary workmanship. It is one of the few volumes out of the many hurriedly issued in the wake of the war which will endure the test of time and stand as a faithful, competent picture to future generations."—Boston *Journal*.

CHARLES SCRIBNER'S SONS, NEW YORK

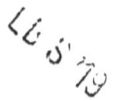

www.ingramcontent.com/pod-product-compliance
Lightning Source LLC
Chambersburg PA
CBHW030812230426
43667CB00008B/1180